THE RAJBANSHIS AND THE GREATER COOCH BEHAR MOVEMENT

THE RAJBANSHIS AND THE GREATER COOCH BEHAR MOVEMENT

SAMARESH BARMAN

ABHIJEET PUBLICATIONS
NEW DELHI 110002

ABHIJEET PUBLICATIONS
4658-A, First Floor, Ambika Bhawan,
21 Ansari Road, New Delhi 110002
Phone: 011-23259444
E-mail: abhijeetpublication@gmail.com
www.abhijeetpublications.com

THE RAJBANSHIS AND THE GREATER COOCH BEHAR MOVEMENT

First Published 2020

ISBN 978-93-88865-47-0

PRINTED IN INDIA

Published by J.K. Singh for Abhijeet Publications, New Delhi-110002, Lasertypeset by Abhijeet Typesetters, New Delhi and Printed at Dynamic Printers, New Delhi.

Dedicated

To the memory of my supervisor (Guide)

Late Professor Tarun Kumar Banerjee

Acknowledgements

This book has grown out of my M.Phil (Master of Philosophy) dissertation submitted to Vidyasagar University in 2017. First of all, I am thankful to my supervisor Professor Tarun Kumar Banerjee (Department of Political Science, Vidyasagar University) for his friendly guidance in the course of writing the Dissertation. Without his constant encouragement, valuable suggestion and critical comments, it would have not been possible to complete the Dissertation. I am also indebted to his timely reminding of my work, sharing his thoughts and reading materials. It is an honor for me to have worked and successfully completed my Dissertation under his guidance and supervision.

I wholeheartedly express my gratitude to Professor Sibaji Pratim Basu (HOD, Department of Political Science, Vidyasagar University) for his intellectual inspiration and friendly support. I should not forget to recall Dr. Ambarish Mukhopadhyay, Dr. Raj Kumar Kothari (Professor, Department of Political Science, VU), Dr. Sujay Ghosh (Associate Professor, Dept. of Political Science, VU), Dr. Eyasin Khan and Dr. Surath

Kumar Malik (Assistant Professor, Dept. of Political Science, VU) for being wonderful teachers and for their constant support and encouragement.

I am grateful to Mr. Alanto Roy, adviser of GCPA, Cooch Behar; Mr. Bablu Adhikary member of GCPA and another member of GCPA, KPP and Rajbanshi peoples whose help give me the data on the history and the problem of Rajbanshis and also their hospitality, kindness, support, and encouragement during my field survey.

Last but not least I shall ever remain grateful to my parents (Bijay Barman and Suniti Barman) and sister (Shyamali Barman) for their love, warmth and unwavering support through the thick and thin of my life.

Any mistakes and errors in the work shall remain mine alone.

Samaresh Barman

Ph.D. Research Scholar,
Department of Political Science,
Raiganj University,
Raiganj, Uttar Dinajpur,
West Bengal.

Contents

List of Abbreviations

AKRSU	- All Koch Rajbanshi Students Union
AKRYCS	- All Assam Koch Rajbanshi Yovo Chatra Sanmilani
AKSO	- All Kamatapur Student's Organization Association
AKSU	- All Kamatapur Student's Union
AGP	- Assam Gana Parishad
BPF	- Bodoland Peoples Front
BJP	- Bharatiya Janata Party
BSF	- Border Security Force
BTC	- Bodoland Territorial Council
CS	- Chilarai Sena
GCBDF	- Greater Cooch Behar Democratic Front
GCPA	- Greater Koch Behar People's Association
GKPF	- Greater Kamatapur Peoples Forum
GOI	- Government of India
HS	- Hitasadhini Sabha

KGP	-	Kamtapur Gana Parishad
KPP	-	Kamtapur Peoples Party
KPP	-	Kamtapuri Progressive Party
KLO	-	Kamatapur Liberation Organization
KRCS	-	Koch Rajbanshi Cultural Society
KRSP	-	Kamta Rajya Sangram Parishad
KRS	-	Koch Rajbanshi Sanmilani
KSP	-	Kamata Sahitya Parishad
KRSS	-	Koch Rajbanshi Sahitya Sabha
NDFB	-	National Democratic Front of Bodoland
NS	-	Narayani Sena
NSCN	-	National Socialist Council of Nagaland
OBC	-	Other Backward Classes
RVA	-	Rajbanshi Vasa Akademi
SC	-	Scheduled Castes
ST	-	Scheduled Tribes
UBSP	-	Uttar Banga Sanskritik Parishad

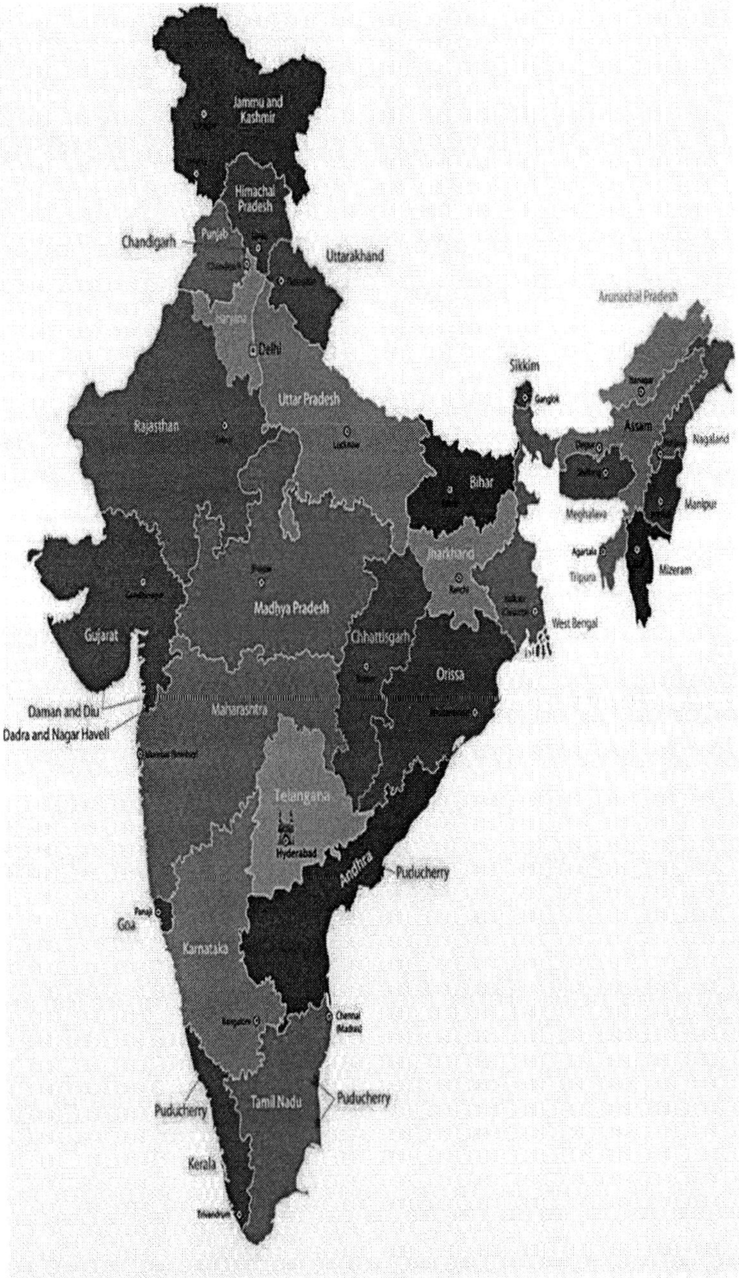

Jammu and Kashmir
Himachal Pradesh
Chandigarh
Punjab
Uttarakhand
Arunachal Pradesh
Delhi
Sikkim
Uttar Pradesh
Rajasthan
Assam
Nagaland
Bihar
Meghalaya
Manipur
Jharkhand
Tripura
Madhya Pradesh
West Bengal
Gujarat
Chhattisgarh
Orissa
Daman and Diu
Dadra and Nagar Haveli
Maharashtra
Telangana
Hyderabad
Andhra
Puducherry
Goa
Karnataka
Puducherry
Tamil Nadu
Puducherry
Kerala

WEST BENGAL

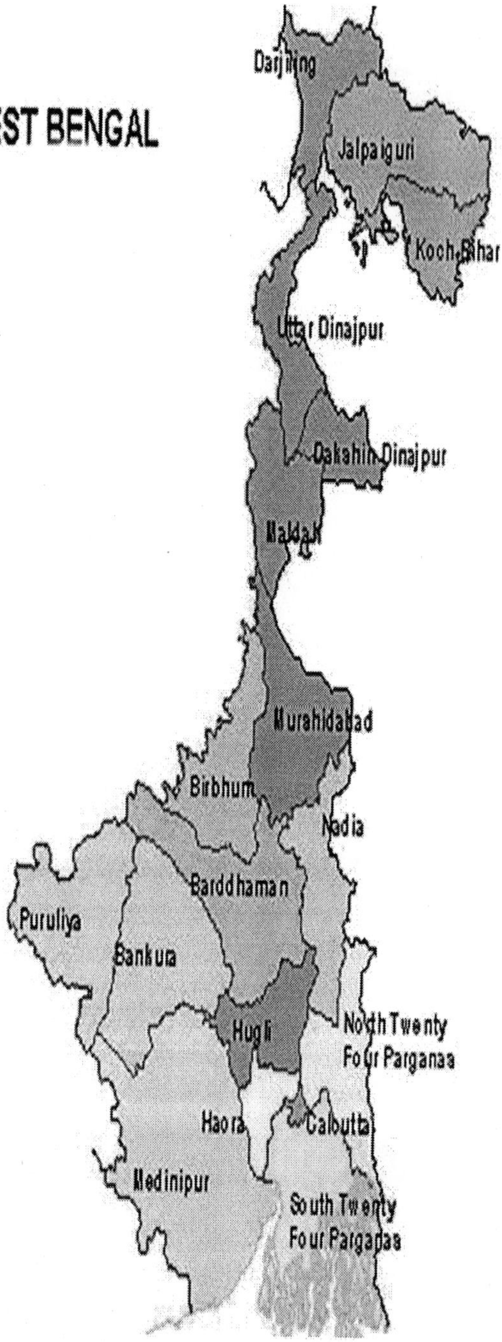
Darjiling
Jalpaiguri
Koch Bihar
Uttar Dinajpur
Dakshin Dinajpur
Maldah
Murshidabad
Birbhum
Nadia
Barddhaman
Puruliya
Bankura
Hugli
North Twenty
Four Parganas
Haora
Calcutta
Medinipur
South Twenty
Four Parganas

Map of Kamatapur/ Greater Cooch Behar

KAMATAPUR

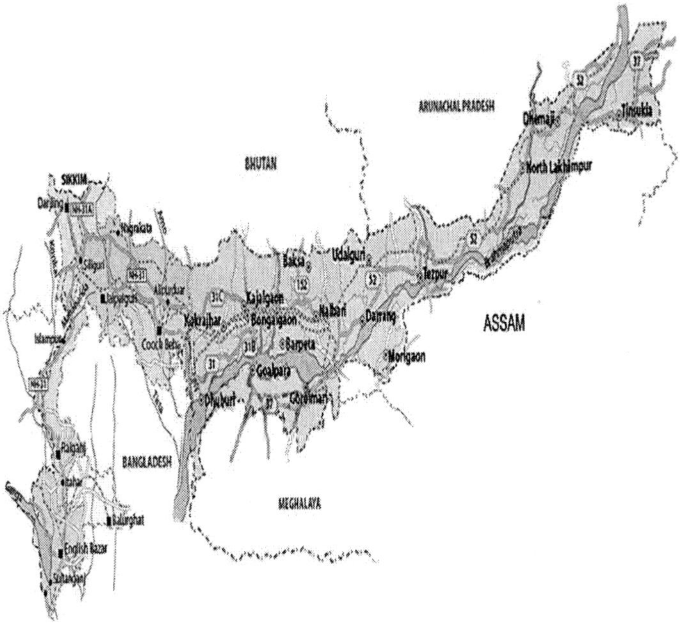

Arts map of Greater Cooch Behar People's Association

Introduction

After 70 years of Indian's independence, access towards basic education, health care facilities housing and potable water poses grave challenges to human survival for the million suffering Indians in the country. Human developments should be pre-requisite of economic development in bridging's the burgeoning gap between 'shining India' and 'survivalist Bharat' is a matter of political will. In the age of globalization, politics and political institutions are ever more central to human development. When the political institutions function badly, poor and vulnerable people suffer most.

Post-independence India is facing new and complex challenges that are diverse from the traditional notion of security challenges. People are living with chronic poverty, acute hunger, and violence, with a lack of basic facilities i.e. food, health, and education. Self-respect and dignity in relation to equality, liberty, and fraternity are still a distant dream for Indian citizens after seven decades of Indian's independence. The rigid and hieranchical social structure, unfinished agenda of land reforms, challenges of caste discrimination and communalism, the problem of women, Tribal and Dalit, the slow pace of reforms, the rise of terrorism and Naxalism are some of the major issues posing challenges to Indians internal security and development.

Separate statehood movement one of the challenges since after independence India. The statehood movement after India's independence got momentum after the framing of a democratic constitution. Many statehood movements took vociferous shape demanding separate state within the Indian union.

This study is as much the study of a movement as it is a study of how a democratically governed state might experience regional disparities existing in various forms. Because issues like this can express its grievances through various means and one amongst them could be a separate state. One can find out many fundamental features of such movement. But one has to be careful while studying the issues of the statehood movement. A large number of statehood movements in India were initially raising the question of economic inequality of regions and alleging discriminations by the developed region within the state.

Gradually when these movements were heading towards their peak the activists of these movements came closely to be associated with many other issues in support of their demands. Significant among them was political discrimination in terms of inadequate representation of leaders from the backward regions in the state council of ministers, attempt of cultural homogenization and in some cases subordination of peripheral culture, language, dialect to mainstream ones.

Colonization and exploitation of natural resources of the backward region is a common phenomenon. The surprising fact is that most of the backward regions in India are ironically rich in mineral resources along with other huge natural resources. When such movements grow and reach their maturity they come to interlink themselves with multiple variables. In some cases, regional movements are identity movements seeking special protection and concessions from the state. It could be a movement for regional self-governance. There are usually two potential and significant causes of the emergence of regional movement-one are the inter-regional or inter-community conflict, and the other is the conflict between the region and the state. In the initial phases of the history of the state formation in India languages played a disproportionate rule.

It may be relevant here to note that the demand of all emerge out of the environment which is an aggregate of a large number of variables like history, geography, soil structure, culture, economy and aspirations of the development of the people. Obviously, the demands of people of one region may differ from the demands of the people of other regions and therefore should be dealt with separately in the regional environmental context, more particularly in a federal polity. In this theoretical backdrop, it is worthwhile to examine the issue of separate statehood. India is a plural polity having different religious and cultural ethos and identities which have well been exploited by the intruders of hues in their own favor, more specifically by the British colonial masters. Acute economic poverty, an exploitative bureaucracy, dismal development, wide-ranging unemployment, illiteracy, malnutrition, etc had been the curse of the colonial rule against which the nationalist forces fought tooth and nail and could free the country from the British tutelage. During the freedom struggle, the leadership assured the masses of all-round development in the post-independence period and as such the father of the Indian Constitution adopted the parliamentary system and federal structure so that people may actively participate in shaping their destiny and putting their might in keeping the nation united and integrated without losing their identity. Keeping this in mind the states were created on linguistic basis. Since our federation is centrifugal and the center had concentrated larger powers in its own hands, it tried to satisfy the developmental needs of the states and sub-regions through institutions like Planning Commissions and National Development Council and the number of programs initiated by it. However, it has been noticed that these plans and programs often fall short to the aspirations of the people of a particular sub-region, since they may not have been implemented so vigorously by the administration. It is due to these reasons that the people of different regions are not satisfied with the form and pace of development. Some regions or sub-regions of the country in recent times have experienced a better economic upswing in comparison with the others. In this backdrop, with the rising level of political consciousness, the people of backward regions started to aspire for more infra-structural growth, better resource mobilization and its use for development in an effort to create an egalitarian social order. However, when their appeals, protests, demands or other related efforts yielded no fruit or marginal success a demand for a separate state emerged. The logic behind such demands has been that the aspirations of the people can only be fulfilled if the administrative power is given to them, by creating a new state.

Separate statehood demanding movements in India:

In recent years, discourses on Indian Federal System are full of controversies. Demand for smaller states has been a very prominent subject and challenges in contemporary Indian politics. Voices for separate statehood have been emerging from different regions, political groups and cultural identities. The creation of new states on regional, linguistic or cultural differences has always been considered to be detrimental and the threat to the unity of the country. Despite strong demands for smaller states, the union government has always dissuaded from the creation of newer states due to susceptibility towards national unity India's experiences with smaller states have demonstrated them to be more efficient and they have shown sing of growth and better governance in comparison to their parental states.

India's diversity in terms of region, language, caste, class, religion, etc makes the issue of identity much more complex. From the pre-colonial and post-colonial period India has experienced many ethnic-based identity conflicts. Despite the division of India resulting in the formation of Pakistan as a separate nation, the country is witnessing the formation of states since the 1950's revolving around the issue of identity. The country also witnessed the emergence of various tribal movements in different parts of the country since the 19th century "of which a few have developed into bitter, violent, and secessionist movements directed against nontribal, against state governments and against the Government of India itself" (Brass: 1999:151). In Punjab, the Khalisthan movement was launched to carve out an independent Sikh country; in Bihar, the Jharkhand movement was directed to preserve the separate tribal identity of Santhals. Likewise, the Gorkhaland movement in West Bengal was motivated by the Gorkha identity issue. The above-mentioned examples reflect the identity assertion movement in India to preserve separate and distinct identity.

Now frame these in a comparative way with reference to various regional movements that are shown in flowing (table no.-1):

Table No.:- 1.

Legacy or Factor	*Movement*	*Form or objective*
1.Pro-British background	i. Dravisthan	Casteist/Secessionist
	ii. Azad Punjab	Communal/Secessionist
	iii. Khashi-Jaintia Federation	Communal/Nativist
	iv. Kshatriya Andolon	Casteist/ Nativist
2.Weak Nationalist Link	i. Dravidaland	Casteist/Secessionist
	ii. Azad Punjab	Ethnic
	iii. Punjabi Sabha	Ethnic Communal
	iv. Jharkhand	Secular/Nativist
	v. Bangla Kheda	Communal/Nativist
	vi. Free Nagaland	Tribal/Secessionist
	vii. Mizo Union	Ethnic Tribal Autonomy
3.Economic Issues	i. Jharkhand	Parochial/Ethnic Development
	ii. Telangana Mulki	Communal/Nativist
	iii. Kamatapuri	Ethnic/Nativist
	iv. Uttarkhand	Secular/Ethnic Existence
	v. Shiva Sena	Ethnic/Nativist

4. Identity	i. Punjabi	Ethnic/Communal
	ii. Khalistan	Domination
	iii. Bangla Kheda	Nativist/Ethnic
	iv. Anti-Foreigners	Domination
	v. Jharkhand	Ethnic/Cultural Resurgence
	vi. Gorkhaland	Ethnic/Nativist Recognization
	vii. Kamatapuri	Nativist/Ethno-Cultural
5. Anti-Outsider sentiment	i. Jharkhand	Economic/Ethno-Development
	ii. Gorkhaland	Ethnic/Nativist
	iii. Mizoram	Nativist/Economic
	iv. Kamatapuri	Economic/Nativist/ Cultural/ Domination
	v. Assam Movement	Economic/Ethnic Domination
6.Area Boundary Disputes	i. Linguistic State Demands	Cultural/Ethnic Solidarity
	ii. Accession of Areas	Economic/Ethnic Linguistic
	iii. Resistance to recognisation	Border Ethno-lingual/Communal
7. Political and Cultural Viz., weak Trade Union movement, weak exposures, Lack of reform.	All the regional sub-regional movements.	Ethno-lingual/ Communal

Source: (Das: 2005:12-13).

The West Bengal Scenario—Rajbanshis and the Greater Cooch Behar Movement:

Cooch Behar is a district of West Bengal, largely populated by the *Rajbanshi* Community. Thus, each community in West Bengal has its own history which has precipitated its identity crisis and led it to the path of movement. *Rajbanshi* is an ethnic community and earliest inhabitant of West Bengal. Historically this community has the features of *Austral-Asiatic, Dravidian, Mongoloid,* and *Aryan*, mixed up with all four human streams or cultures but Mongoloid features were pre-dominant (Roy: 2007:09).

Usually, this community has been living in whole of North Bengal barring its hilly terrains; in a sizable portion of Assam; western part of Meghalaya; Purnia, Kishanganj districts and eastern part of Katihar district of Bihar; Jhapa and Biratnagar districts of Nepal; Rangpur, east Dinajpur district and some parts of northwest Mymensingh, northern Rajshahi and Bogra districts of present-day Bangladesh and lower parts of Bhutan. They are known as *Rajbanshi Kshatriya* Bengali in North Bengal, simply Rajbanshi in Bihar and Nepal and as *Koch Rajbanshi* in Assam, Meghalaya and their adjoining areas (Roy: 2007:08). The Koch Kingdom ruled in Kamatapur and it is said that Sandhya Rai established the Kingdom of Kamata in the 13th century including few portions of North Bengal and West Assam of present Northeast India. The kingdom of Kamata was ruled by different rulers of different dynasties from the period of the mid 13th century to the end of the 15th century (Das: 2009:38-39). The Koch established their strong political power in the Kamata region in the early 16th century by the Koch Chieftain *Bishwa Singha* (1515-1540). After the death of *Bishwa Singha*, many other Koch Kings ruled the Kamatapur region till the treaty of April 5, 1773, signed between King Dharmendra Narayan and East India Company. Through this treaty Kamatapur alias, Cooch Behar became a native state of British India and continued till 1947. In West Bengal District

Gazetteers Durgadas Majumder writes that until 28th August 1949 Cooch Behar was an Indian State ruled by *Maharaja Jagadipendra Narayan* under British Government. By a document on 28th August 1949, Maharaja Jagaddipendra Narayan gave up his territory to the Government of India. By an order under section 290A of the Government of India Act 1935, Cooch Behar Behar was included and merged with West Bengal on 1st January 1950. Since then it is being administered as a district of West Bengal (Das: 2009:56).

This community has been subject to a feeling of an identity crisis, discriminatory attitudes of state government as well as very poor socio-economic condition. Naturally due to all the political representation is very low compared to the people of other community. Against this backward, the Rajbanshis have been engaged in a political movement and demand of separate state of Greater Cooch Behar.

Originally the movement started under the leadership of Thakur Panchanan Barma. During those times Rajbanshis did not like to mention themselves as '*Koch*' which was considered as the inferior term. Under the leadership of Haramohan Khajanchi, Harikishor Barman and afterward under Thakur Panchanan Barma and Upendra Nath Barman, the people organized 'Kshatriya Andolan (1910)' and claimed '*Kshatriyahood*' for themselves. But the Movement could not process successfully due to certain reasons.

After the independence, an intellectual section of the Rajbanshi Community mainly from the Cooch Behar district came under the umbrella of a new non-political organization called "*Greater Cooch Behar People's*

Association (GCPA)" in 1998 with a declared objective for the welfare of people of Cooch Behar and placed a demand for separate statehood. *Uttar Khanda Dal (UKD)* an organization was born in 1969, demanding a separate state for Rajbanshis namely as Kamtapur or Uttar Khanda. *'Uttar Banga Sanskritik Parishad'* another organization formed in the same year also raised the demand for recognition of Kamta language and its development. A similar organization named *Kamta Rajya Sangram Parishad (KRSP)* was formed in the Goalpara district of Assam in 1969. For the same purpose in 1987, UKD changed its name to Kamtapur Gana Parishad and in 1996 to *Kamtapur Peoples Party (KPP)* (Ray: 2007:116). Kamatapur Liberation Organisation (KLO), a militant organization came into being on 28th December 1995. *All Koch Rajbanshi Students Union (AKRSU)* and *Koch Rajbanshi Sanmilani (KRS)* are the two Assam based organization fighting for separate Kamatapur state and Schedule Tribe status for the Koch Rajbanshis living in Assam. Their proposed Kamatapur state comprises of eleven districts of Assam and five districts of North Bengal. A faction of this party formed another regional Ethno cultural-political parties like Kamatapuri Pragatishil Party, Greater Cooch Behar Democratic Front and Kamatapur Progressive Party, etc. come on a common platform and continue the statehood demand. With this background, the proposed study is an attempt to understand the historical process of Rajbanshis identity formation and the historical memory of the Kamatapur state in the cultural and political life of Rajbanshis; the problem of identity among them from the pre-independence to the post-independence period; and the roots and causes of their long-drawn ethnic identity movement and the strategies carried out by them to resolve identity crisis.

Socio-economic condition and political representation is an important indicator to measure the development level of any community. The condition of Rajbanshi people will not be improved by demanding a separate state. It may only be possible by improving socio-economic factors like- education (by giving more schools and colleges), health (by giving more facilities in hospitals and establishing more rural health centers), and infrastructures such as roads, electricity, banking facilities, and agro-based industries. In fact, all the district of North Bengal is industrially backward. In agriculture, Cooch Behar is in a good position. But there is no such agro-based industry where the number of unemployed young and middle-aged can engage them. To improve the socio-economic situation of this province a thorough investigation to find out the nature of disparities is required.

The planning of this book is as follows. The first introductory to explain briefly the concept of separate statehood movement, the process of ethnic identity formation and periphery of the few cases separate statehood movement, identity crisis and conflict in contemporary India and relation it with that of Rajbanshi in West Bengal. Then the first chapter has been explored the origin of the Rajbanshi community identity and historical memory of Kamatapur state viz to viz history of Cooch Behar State in the cultural and political life of Rajbanshis. This chapter fully elaborated on Cooch Behar Kingdom's history. This chapter finally, discusses the merger agreement with Cooch Behar State and Indian Union and unfortunately,

Cooch Behar merges in West Bengal and origin the separate statehood movement. In the second chapter has been analyzed the short biography of Panchanana Barma. After I discuss in this chapter will Panchanana Barma's impact Kshatriya movement, women empowerment and education, Kshatriya Bank and many reforms of the Rajbanshi Communities. The third chapter have look into the origin and objectives of the separate statehood movement among Rajnbanshi, the socio-economic-political agitation identity crisis, and their demands. This chapter will also study political mobilization among the Rajbanshi community in encountering the many problems. Further, the chapter will explain the state government and central government towards the socio-political movements of Rajbanshi.

Finally, I did sum up the entire findings of the study on the basis of discussion and I suggest some probable solution to the problems. In addition, the limitation of the study and scope for further research also explained.

REFERENCES

Brass, Paul R. (1999), *Ethnicity and Nationalism: Theory and Comparison*, Sage Publication, New Delhi.

Das, Arup Jyoti (2009), *Kamatapur and Koch Rajbanshi Imagination*, Arunima Deka Publication, Guwahati.

Das, Dhirendra Nath (2005), *Regional Movements, Ethnicity and Politics*, Abhijeet Publications, Delhi.

Roy, Nalini Ranjan (2007), *Koch Kingdom and Kamatapur: The Truth Univeiled*, Vicky Publication, Guwahati.

1

Historical Background of the Greater Cooch Behar Movement

From the 5th of July 1969, the Rajbanshis of West Bengal (W.B.) started a vigorous mass movement demanding a separate state in the Tista-Brahmaputra valley under the leadership of *Uttar Khanda Dal (UKD)* (Barman: 2007:129-130). The movement attracted nation-wide attention with both its integrationist and secessionist assertions. Hence a complete understanding of the movement becomes important. While discussing the causes it has to be kept in mind that the *Kamatapur/ Greater Cooch Behar movement* did not take place due merely to the existence of cultural differences nor for the socio-political domination and subordination by the culturally different ethnic Bengalis and Assamese. Certain circumstances and events within the community affected the collective existence of Rajbanshi people leading finally to a massive assertion. This chapter aims to unveil the background and immediate circumstance leading to the Greater Cooch Behar movement for a separate state.

Before discussing the immediate circumstances of the Greater Cooch Behar movement a brief history of the Rajbanshis community in the Tista-Brahmaputra valley of Northern Bengal and Western Assam in necessary.

The Origins of the Rajbanshis:

The history of the Rajbanshi people is shrouded is a mystical fact. The Rajbanshis were the people of the greater part of North Bengal and lower Assam, the majority Rajbanshis people were live in North Bengal, particularly in the district of Cooch Behar, Jalpaiguri, Dinajpur (North and South) and the plain area of Darjeeling district. The Rajbanshi many people live in Bangladesh (Rangpur, East Dinajpur, North-Western part of Mymensingh district), lower Bhutan Assam (Goalpara, northern part of Kamrup and Western part of Naogaon district), Meghalaya, Nepal (Bhadrapur and Jhapa, Morang district), Eastern part of Purnea district of Bihar, some parts of Tripura. The 1921 Census Report displays about 89% of the Rajbanshi population lived in the only district i.e. Cooch Behar, Jalpaiguri, Dinajpur, and Rangpur (Census of India: 1921:358).

Swaraj Basu explained that "... The Rajbanshis constituted the most predominant section of the local Hindu population in the Northern districts of Bengal. The origin of Rajbanshi caste is shrouded in mystery and the basic debate is around the question of their association with the Koches. Whatever might have been their actual origin? There is no dispute about the fact that the Rajbanshis were the early settlers in North Bengal. They were a socially homogenous community, in the sense that there was no sub-caste among them" (Basu: 2003:15).

There are many viewpoints among the origin or ethnological identity of the Rajbanshi. The main viewpoint or debate was whether Rajbanshis were originated from the *Mongoloid race or Aryan race*. Some scholars elaborated, "the Rajbanshis are of Kshatriya or Aryan origin, and they have subsequently become fallen down and made themselves known as Rajbanshis, the term signifying their association with the *Raja* (King) and on the other hand the Koch tribe of Bodo origin. The basis of this standpoint is that the Cooch Behar dynasty, which ruled in Kamrup, had their origin from Koch Tribe. The king and the subjects being of some stock in this region, the Rajbanshis belong to the Koch". Both approaches deserve some amount of discussions.

I discuss are different work for official and non-official on the origin question of Rajbanshis. Broadly, there are two lines of arguments as to the origin of the Rajbanshis, one hand the colonial official-cum-ethnographers and other hands the Rajbanshis caste publicists and indigenous literature like Ramayana, Mahabharat, Puranas, and Tantra Scriptures etc.

The very first proper ethnographic details were documented by colonial ethnographers of erstwhile British Empire who aimed at scientifically documenting various caste and tribal groups. Buchanan Hamilton in his reports, *"Accounts of the District of Rangpur 1810"* compacted in that book gives an account for the history of the Rajbanshi. He elaborated in his report Koch and Rajbanshis both being part of the larger Bodo stock and the same caste. The report still says that not all the Rajbanshis are Koches. Although most of them are those who have become degenerated by adopting the profession of palanquin bearer Koch and amongst them, those who have become further degraded by taking to the habits of eating pork, chicken, etc. are Dahoi or Garol. (Hamilton: 1810)

B.H. Hadgson elaborated in his report that Biswa Singh's grandfather Hajo founded the Koch Kingdom. Hajo and his grandson Biswa Singh became Hindu, renounced the name Koch and adopted Rajbanshi. Hadgson says that Koch and Kuvaca are synonyms. He had divided for the Assam Koch were three types- (a) *Kamthali*, (b) *Madai*, (c) *Kolita* and Rangpur Koch were two types- (a) *Rajbanshi* and (b) *Koch*. (Hadgson: 1849:704-706)

L.A. Waddel says that the Rajbanshis do not belong to the Dravidian stock, "but are distinctly Mongoloid though somewhat heterogeneous". This view supported Hadgson. L.A. Waddel writing:

> "This term 'Koch' has become more of a caste title than a tribal appellation so that individuals of the Kacharie, Garo, Rabha, Lalung and allied Indo-Chins tribes are admitted as members and there seems also in places to be slight learning with Nama Sudra blood. Thus any one of these tribes can become a Koch by establishing a Brahmanical ritual and giving up eating beef. In this stage, he is called 'Saraniya', and 'Horoniy' (usually pronounced in the Assam fashion), which means 'a refugee', implying that he has taken refuge in Hinduism. The more advanced stage can be gained leaving off beef and swine's

> flesh and strong drink altogether when he assumes the full externals and status of a Hindu ... only assign by the more orthodox Hindu the position of one of the very lowest caste. The term Koch, therefore, not being a favored one in Bengali it is usual to find then dropping that title wherever there is a resident Raja of their own Kindred as at 'Koch Bihar' (Cooch Behar), Darang, Bijni, Mech para, Sidli, Beltola, Jalpaiguri and Lakhi. At such places, they call themselves by the higher sounding Indian title Rajbanshi or Royal Race" (Waddel: 1975:48).

E.T. Dalton suggested that the Rajbanshis were related to the neighboring Koch, Mechs, Garo and the Bodo-Kachari tribes but underwent a lot of admixtures to develop into a district community: "The Rajbanshi are all very dark and as their cognates, the Kacharis, Mechs, Garos are yellow or light brown and their northern, eastern and western neighbors are as fair of fairer, it must be form contact with the people of the south that they got their black skin". He elaborated that the Rajbanshis are belongings to non-Aryan stock and Bodo population based on their physical appearances. He considers the Rajbanshi as belonging to the Dravidian stock. (Dalton: 1872:89-93)

Captain Lewis, a Deputy Commissioner of Cooch Behar while commenting on the Census of 1872, "The present inhabitants of Cooch Behar State do not belong to any particular race. The Meches who inhabit the Bhutan Duars coming into a compact with the immigrants from the south intermarriage have taken place and the descents are the modern Cooch Beharis" (Choudhury: 1903:125).

Dr. W.W. Hunter explained that on the close of the fifteenth century one Koch King Hajo established the Kingdom of Kamrup. Hajo's grandson Bishwa Singh including with his officers and all people of the condition apostatized to Hindu. A divine ancestry for chief was manufactured by the Brahmins. The converts abandoned the name Koch and took that of Rajbanshi (Hunter: 1876:402). Hunter also describes that Cooch Behar, Jalpaiguri, and Rangpur, the name Rajbanshi, which literally means *'Royal Race'*, is adopted by the agriculturist and respectable men, that of Koch being restricted to laborers and especially to the palanquin bearers (Hunter: 1876:347-348).

Herbert Risley in the same way marked:

> "Rajbanshi, Paliya, Deshi, Koch, Koch-Mandi are large Dravidian tribes of North-East and Eastern Bengal among who there is ground for suspecting some admixture of Mongoloid blood. Today the name Koch, without doubt, the original designation of the districts where they are most many and where there is very reason to believe them to represent the earliest permanent settlers. The Koch was the transformation into the Rajbanshi. The Rajbanshi is now known in Rangpur, Cooch Behar, Jalpaiguri is a singular example of the influence exercised by fiction in the making of caste. Now the great majority of the Koch Tribes resident

of Northern Bengal invariably describe themselves as Rajbanshi or Bhanga-Kshatriya; a denomination that enables them to pose as an outgoing branch of the Kshatriyas who fled to these remote districts in order to escape from the wrath of Parsuram. Rajbanshi people claim that they are disembarked from King (Raja) Dasarath, father of Rama. They keep Brahmans, being the Brahmanical ritual in their marriage ceremony. They have begun to adopt the Brahmanical system in gotras (Kasyapa). The original nucleus of the Rajput group may have been Aryan that of the Rajbanshi was certainly Dravidian. Herbert Risley also says that the Rajbanshi, Paliya, Koch, Desi and other varieties by whatever names they are descended from a Dravidian stock. They have brought under control the valley of the Ganges at the time of the Aryan advance into Bengal driven forward by this incursion into the swamps and forests of Northern and North-Eastern Bengal. The tribes were and there brought into contact with the Mongoloid races of the lower Himalayas and of the Assam, border and their type may have affected to a varying degree by intermixture with these people. Overall Dravidian characteristics predominate among them over Mongolian (Risley: 1891:491-492).

O'Malley describes that "the Rajbanshi or Barua Mugs are the offspring of Bengali woman by Burmese men or more generally of Arakanes mothers by Bengali fathers" (O'Malley: 1911:399). He also told that "a most persistent agitation was carried on by Rajbanshis of North Bengal with the object of being recognized as Ksatriyas by decent. They desired not only to be recorded separately from Koch but also distinguished by the name Ksatriyas. The former request was granted without hesitation as there is no doubt that at the present day, irrespective of any question of origin, the Rajnbanshi and the Koch are separate castes. It was however out of the question to allow them to be returned the generic and archaic name of Kshatriya" (O'Malley: 1911:445).

W.H. Thomson explained, "The Rajbanshis are indigenous people of North Bengal and the Third Largest Hindu caste in the province. Rajbanshis total number has been exaggerated by the fact that a member of the fisherman caste in Mymensingh, Nadia and Murshidabad returned themselves as Rajbanshi. May of the Rajbanshis have taken sacred thread and were prepared to use force in support of their claim to be returned as Kshatriya" (Thomson: 1921:358). He also writes, "No part of the Census in 1891, 1901, 1911 aroused so much excitement as the return of caste which caused a great deal heart burning and in some were returned as Kshatriya quarters with treats of disturbance of the peace" (Thomson: 1921:346-349).

A.E. Porter says, "Some more gotras other than Kashyapa were introduced amongst the Rajbanshis. They are- (i) *Kashyapa*, (ii) *Sandilya*, (iii) *Bharedwaja*, (iv) *Goutama*, (v) *Savarna*, (vi) *Kapila*, (vii) *Thandi*, (viii)

Batsya, (ix) *Maudgala*, (x) *Arti*, (xi) *Parasar*, (xii) *Kausuka*, (xiii) V*iswamitra*". Then he comments, "the Rajbanshis have now to some extent regularized the anomalous position in which they found themselves until recently owing to the fact upon assumption of the Kshatriya status they had all adopted themselves into some gotras (Kashyapa) with the result that all marriage amongst Rajbanshi as Kshatriya would, upon a strict interpretation of Hindu law have invalid owing to their being within the same gotras." "But even amongst those families which have been invested with sacred tread, it is apparently only the literate section who claim to belong to any gotras and those, when it is necessary to disclose a gotras at all, plum for the kashyapa gotras as a matter of course"(Porter: 1931:474).

A.E. Porter also describes that "Rajbanshi, Koch, Palia were the same originally. The Kaivarttas of Assam and North Bengal has more affinity with Rajbanshis. They all claimed to be recorded a Rajbanshis and all the Rajbanshis claimed to be recorded as Kshatriyas at the beginning of the 19th century. The more backward and illiterate members of the Rajbanshis caste still maintain practices inconsistent with orthodox Hindu belief" (Porter: 1931:473).

H. Beverly comments that the Rajbanshis, Koch and Palias had a common origin but also stated that Rajbanshi is not a term exclusive to Northern Bengal. He says, "The Koch, Paliya, and Rajbanshi are for the most part one and the same tribe... Rajbanshi is an indefinite term and some few individuals entered under if many possibly belong to other castes. In the lower delta, for instance, Rajbanshis is said to be a subdivision of Tiyars, but by for the great majority of those returned as such coming as Rajbanshi from the districts of Dinajpur, Rangpur, Jalpaiguri, Cooch Behar, and Goalpara are clearly the same as Koch and Paliyas who are found in those districts"(Berevly:1872:130).

Charu Chandra Sanyal writes "the Kochs are non-Aryan origin. Some of them adopted Hinduism and became Rajbanshis. These Rajbanshis, later on, claimed to be kshatriyas. There has been controversy regarding marriage within one Gotra. It is true that a Hindu male cannot marry a girl of the same Gotra or Pravara. This rule does not apply to the Sudras who are said to have no Gotra of their own, but it applies to the Kshatriyas and the Vaisyas although it is alleged that neither of them has any Gotra nor Pravara of their own. The Gotra of these castes is said to be those of the gurus of preceptors or the priests of their ancestors. These gurus or preceptors are probably the same as *'Paruas'* of the Rajbanshi (Sanyal: 1965:13).

On the other hand in the indigenous literature referred to the Rajbanshis were as different from and superior (in rank) to the Koch. So many number scholar and writers elaborated that Rajbanshi and Koch are different castes and Rajbanshi are upper (*Kshatriya*) class in Hindu. For example, Nalini Ranjan Roy elaborated that the ancestors of the Rajbanshi were settlers in the semi-hilly terrains and plains of present-day North Bengal, Assam, and their adjoining areas. They embraced the Aryan culture and later took to Hinduism. Hinduism denoted the way of civilized life, following of Vedic procedures of rituals and adoption of *'Sanskritised'* Maithili Apabhramsa languages, which Aryan culture brought along with its advent into this part of ancient India. He writes:

> "The people of this community have the features mixed up with all four human streams i.e. Austral-Asiatic or 'Adivasi', Dravidian, Mongoloid and Aryan, where the Mongoloid features like height, fair complexion and having flat nose are predominant. Some of them can be seen as tall, fare and having sharp nose like people of north or midland Indians, who trace their origin in Aryan culture; some of them can be seen as far as Aryan people and at the same time some as dark complexion as Adivasis or Dravidians. This region was like a eastern gateway of India or a meeting place where all four human streams got amalgamated, which gave birth to new '*Sanskritised*' culture of the northeastern part of India" (Roy:2007:9-10)

Monomohan Roy stated, "Inspections of any question as to identify or difference of origin the Rajbanshis and Koches from entirely distinct castes." In social status, the Koches were inferior to the Rajbanshis, who had greater ceremonial purity than the Koches did. The physical features of the great majority of the Rajbanshis of Rangpur, Cooch Behar, and Jalpaiguri were distinctly 'Dravidian'. The physiognomy of the Koches was decided 'Mongoloid'. He also told that the distinction between the Rajbanshiand the Koches in the Rangpur district is not of recent growth, but points to a real ethnological difference. The theory that the term Rajbanshi is merely a recent title of the Koch who assumed it on the establishment of the Kingdom of Cooch Behar does not on a close examination of the existing facts; appear to be a tenable one (Roy: 1902:50-53).

In contract to received narrative based primarily on the colonial accounts, Swaraj Basu describes consensus among scholars regarding the obscure origins of the Rajbanshi as a distinct ethnic group and uses this as a starting place for addressing the complexities hidden within the discourse. He elaborated that understanding Rajbanshi origins are essentially liked to who are or were, the Koch in relation to the Rajbanshi. He uses three contradictory quotes from historical and colonial accounts to demonstrate this point:

> "The Koch and the Rajbanshi did not belong to the same caste, they were different castes. The Rajbanshis were superior to the Koches. Their origins were also different and different were their occupations" (Basu: 2003:25).

Hari Kishore Adhikary also says that the Koches and the Rajbanshis were not the same castes and they were different in many ways. The behavior, culture, food habits are the upper caste Hindu including the Rajbanshis. Adhikary told stressed that the Rajbanshis are upper caste which is borne out, by their food habits, behavior, and customs. The Rajbanshis celebrated all their ceremonies and ritual in the fashion of the Kshatriyas and another upper-caste Hindus. He also objected to the argument that the Rajbanshis adopted Hinduism during the region of Maharaja

Biswa Singha of the Cooch Behar in the early 16th century. He says the Rajbanshis were Hindus before the region of Biswa Singha and were recognized as Bhanga Kshatriyas. According to the Shastra's term, Bhanga Kshatriya had no meaning so they had come recognized as 'Rajbanshi' (Adhikary: 1907:21-25).

Upendra Nath Barman also says in the same way that the Rajbanshis were Kshatriya and lived in the land "*Pundra Desh*" between the river Karotoya and Gangs. He unproved the view of colonial ethnographers by citing an example from the Hindu Shastras and Puranas and he says that Rajbanshis were claiming the *Kshatriya* status long before the eighteenth century (Barman: 1941:01-55).

Hiuen Tsang and S. K. Chatterjee have observed that the whole of Bengal including the Northern part adopted the Aryan language and culture by the 7th century. While assuming the views for some difference between the language of Kamrup and that of Middle India, as alluded by Hiuen Tsang, he has said that Kamatapuri language has Tibeto-Burman elements and as such the Aryan language has been a bit distorted by Kamrup pronunciation (Barma: 2004:66).

S.K. Chatterjee adopted that the language of North Bengal was principally the Aryan language in the 7th century itself. Unfortunately, he had adopted two contradictory positions as reflected from his observations mentioned above. From the statement of the track followed by Baqtiar Khalji for his Tibet invasion in *Tabakat-i-Nasiri*, as mention by Sukumar Das in Uttar Banger Ittihas. It clears that Baqtiar Khalji and his followers contact the mountainous tribes and their language and there was no opportunity of their contact with the people of the Plains, i.e. Rajbanshi (Das: 1982:103-104).

The History of the Rajbanshis for the other sources is indigenous literature like are the *Ramayana, the Mahabharata, Puranas, Up-Pranas, Tantras,* etc.

According to *Bhramari Tantra:*

Nandisuta Bhayadbhime Poundradesat samgatah

Bardhanasya Panchputrah Swaganairbandhabaih saha

Ratnapithan Bibasante Kaladbriprara Sangamat

Kshatra Drarmaparakranta Rjbanshti khyata bhube.

(*Bhramaritantra*: 2nd Stanza).

Meaning the above lines are: "out of fear from the son of Nandi i.e. (Mahapadma Nanda) the five sons of Bardhana including Bhimeshwara with their relatives come from Poundradesh and settled down in Ratnapitha of Kamrup and for a long time duc to disconnection with Brahmans being derailed from Kshatriya rituals, become known as Rajbanshi in the earth.

According to *Kalika Purana:*

Jamadagnya bhayabhitah Kshatriya Purbamebahi

Mleccha Chandmanu Pudaya Jalpisam Sarnam gatah.

Te Mlecch bachah Satatamaryabachsha Sarbada

Jalpaisam Sebamanaste gopayanti cha tang haram.

(*Tarkaratan:* 1384 BS:95-125).

The above line says that out of fear from the son of Jamadagni i.e. (*Pasuram*) the person who was previously known as Kshatriyas assuming the garb and matre of Mlecchas settled down round about Jalpesh (now today Jalpesh is located in Maynaguri subdivision of Jalpaiguri district). They who always used both Mecchas and Aryan speeches use to worship *Lord Siva* Secretly.

As a of Mahapurusa Sankardeva Pandit Rupnanarayana in his *'Kamateshwar Kula Kalika'* writes:

Mahanadisuta nanda Bouddharaja Sandamanda
Dhbansa Kare Kshatrabansha tin Saptabar.
Seha gota bhujabale yujhilen abhele
Dbiteeya Parashuram Jitu Abatar
Chhiriye gulardari kshatri Chinya lupta kari
Pranbhayae iti uti Palanta Sakali.
Sangramak bhaya kari bhanga Kshatri nama dhari
Apnake mane keha Rajbanshi buli.
Bardhana suta Panchjan Ratnapithe nila than
Arakeha lukaila Yonigarbhapithe
Taramadhye Bhemeswara Aradhila Maheswware
Siddha haila sita Ratnapither nikate.

Means: The second Parsurama, the son of Nandi demolished the Kshatriyas for 21 (twenty-one) time. In addition, the Kshatriyas, being afraid of war, tore of the sacred sacrificial thread and took the name as Bhanga Kshatriya and some of them as Rajbanshi (some of them sense as Rajbanshi). The five sons of Bardhana including Bhimeswara lived in Ratanapitha. Bhimeswara has worshipped Siva and he succeeded in penance near Rathnapitha.

The ancient history of the Rajbanshis, their living place was Kamrupa. Ancient kamrup had four parts– viz. *Kampitha, Yonipitha, Manipitha, and Ratnapitha*. The most western part of the Kingdom was Ratnapith, where live-in Rajbanshi. Yogini Tantra and the account of Buchanan Hamilton also supported this view. From this point of view the boundary of ancient Kamrupa and the present location of Jalpesh in Maynaguri police station of Jalpaiguri district, that the location of Ratnapitha and Jalpesh is the same.

According to the Puranic account, the origin of the name *'Pundra'* as ascribed to one of the five sons of the Asura King Bali. R.C. Majumder also supports this view (Majumder: 2011:120). He writes they lived in North Bengal popularly known as pundradesh and Pundra Vardhan one of the famous cities in ancient times. Mahastangarh located at a place with a distance of seven miles from Bogra. This argument of R. C. Majumder as well accepted now. According to Manu Samhita Poundra, Odra, Kamboja, Yavana, Soka, and Kirata all these Kshatriya people have degraded to Sudra because of the *Brahamans*. In the annotation of Sloka 44 of Chapter 10 (ten) of Manu Samhita, kulluk commented that Kshatriyas who used to live in pundra vardhana abandoned the Vedic rites and got degenerated to Sudra.

From the ancient period Rajbanshi people accents to the Aryan languages and culture by the 7th century. Itself adopted the Indo-Aryan language as their own. However, from the standpoint of religions and culture, the process of assimilations is continuing. It is from this angle that the Rajbanshi claim the *Kshatriyas*. The claim that Koches and Rajbanshi are not the same they tried to prove their Kshatriya status by taking the sacred thread to get rib the degradation.

The Rajbanshi organized mass agitation from time to time to identify themselves as the descendants of

Aryan and tried to establish their Kshatriya identity in government records. It took quite a well-organized shape towards the end of the 19th century and the beginning of the 20th century. Finally, the Rajbanshi became successful to recognize themselves as *'Kshatriya'* in the final record of the 1911 Census, where they were listed as a separate Hindu caste *'Rajbanshi'* with Kshatriya in bracket (Barman: 1941:18-19).

In the time of the Census operations of 1921 and 1931, the Rajbanshis once again mobilized the community and appalled to the Census authority to return them as only Kshatriya in place of Raajbanshi Kshatriya. Panchanan Barma (1866-1935) was born of the village Khalishamari of Mathabhanga subdivision of Cooch Behar district and a leader of the Rangpur Court was the Chief architect of this agitation towards its final stage. He sacrificed in his life in this community reforms (Singha: 2011:42-52).

Although there is a difference in opinion it can be very well said that the Rajbanshis belong to the Aryan race as per their religious beliefs, rites, social manners and customs, speech and their physical features. But in due course of time with the gradual intermixture with the Mongoloid, it paved the way for the evolution of a mixed type- the Aryan-Mongoloid (also Dravidian) type in which the characteristic feature of both races was found.

Constitutionally speaking, the Rajbanshis are registered as general caste in Nepal, OBC (Other Backward Caste) in Assam Scheduled Caste (SC) in West Bengal and Scheduled Tribe (ST) in Meghalaya. Identify select communities for special development privileges, the SC list includes the names of those castes considered to be outside the Classical Hindu Varna system, but still falling within the general purview of the Hindu religion. The Koch, often recognized as a central group thus engendering the Koch-Rajbanshi sub-group, are also recognized in the SC list, but separate from the Rajbanshi. Furthermore, the Indian Constitution scheduled tribes (ST) that, despite syncretic elements in religious belief and practice, are deemed to be entirely outside the Hindu belief system due to their loyalties to different customs and pantheon of gods. The Rajbanshi have never been included in the ST list despite efforts by a number of Activist organizations, including the Kamatapur Liberation Organization (KLO), the Greater Cooch Behar Peoples' Association, KPP, AKRSU, AKSU, and prominent leaders and intellectuals claim ST status for them.

The Short History of Kamatapur and the Cooch Behar Kingdom

In studying the ancient process of Rajbanshi identity composition and their statehood movement it is very much important to study the history of Kamatapur kingdom 13th century onward. Kamatapur was a region where the Rajbanshi kingdom ruled over for a long time period. In the present social and political discourse, the Rajbanshis feel proud to identify themselves with Kamatapuri. The present socio-political movement for separate Kamatapur or Greater Cooch Behar state draws its inspiration from the historical memory of Kamatapur. History told that Rajbanshi kingdom was there in the Kamatapur for a long time period from the 13th century onwards and disappeared in the process of after independent state formation in India with the Indian state of West Bengal, Assam and some part in Bangladesh. Now today it is noticed that the Rajbanshis of West Bengal particularly in North Bengal and Assam particularly west Assam identify them as Kamatapuri and therefore today demand Greater Cooch Behar (Kamatapur) state also seeks recognition of the history and culture of Kamatapur.

Kamatapur was very much there in the history from 13th century onwards. Even when Hiuen Tsang, the famous traveler, and scholar from China visited the ancient Kamarupa kingdom of Bhashkar Barma from between 606 to 648 A.D. the capital of Kamrup was believed to be Kamatapur. What we find in "*A History of Assam*" is that, '[T]here were at this point (during the reign of Bhaskar Burma) no larger towns, and the capital of the country does not appear to have been a place of much importance. The only indication that is given as to its locality is that it lay 150 miles east of Paundra Vardhana. Cunningham, after identifying the later place with Pabna, concluded that it was at Kamatapur (Gait: 2011:26). Many times Kamatapur has appeared as the capital of the Kamata kingdom in the history of Northeast India. And sometimes Kamata and Kamrup have been treated as the same kingdom. According to Edward Gait, the Muhammadan historians sometimes speak as if the terms Kamrupa and Kamata were synonymous and applicable to one and the same country, but on the other occasions they appear to regard them as distinct, and it would seem that at times the tracts east and west of the Sankosh owed allegation to different rulers, just as they did in the later days of Rajbanshi rule (Gait: 2011:42-43).

Sandhya Rai established the Kingdom of Kamata in the 13th century comprising few portions of North Bengal and West Assam of present Northeast India. Historian N.N. Acharyya has written a brief chapter on the Kingdom of Kamata in his book *"A Brief History of Assam"*. He writes, "Shortly after the invasion of Kamrup by Tughril Khan Malik Yuzbeg, the capital of Kamrup was transferred by king Sandhya from 'Kamrup Nagar' (North Guwahati) to Kamatapur (Cooch Behar) in the west. From that time onward, the Kingdom of Kamrup was known as 'Kamata' or Kamrup- Kamata. The rulers of Kamata were designated as *Kamateshwara or Kameswara* (*Lord of Kamata*). The kingdom of Kamata became, however, much smaller in extent than ancient Kamrup. It included Dhubri, Goalpara, Kokrajhar, Barpeta, Nalbari, and Kamrup district of modern Assam, besides portions of northern Bengal (Cooch Behar, Jalpaiguri, Darjeeling, Uttar Dinajpur, and Dakin Dinajpur) and Mymensingh (Bangladesh). ...." (Acharyya:1996:42). R. N. Ray writes "the geographically contiguous areas of Barendra-Pundra-Kamta-Kamrup comprising of the whole of present-day North Bengal, Northern district of Bihar, Jhapa-Biratnagar region of eastern Nepal, Rajbanshi division of Bangladesh, Western Assam, lower parts of Bhutan and some parts of Meghalaya were parts of Kamrup"(Roy: 2007:13). F. B. Hamilton in his Manuscripts writs "the Boundaries of Kamrup almost the whole of it is included in the ancient Hindu territory of Kamrup, which extends east from the Korotoya where it joined by the Kingdom of Motsyo to Dikorbasini, a river in Assam which enters the Brahmaputra a little to the East of the eastern Kamakhya. The southern boundary of Kamrup is where

Figure: - 1: Some Maps of Ancient Kamatapur State

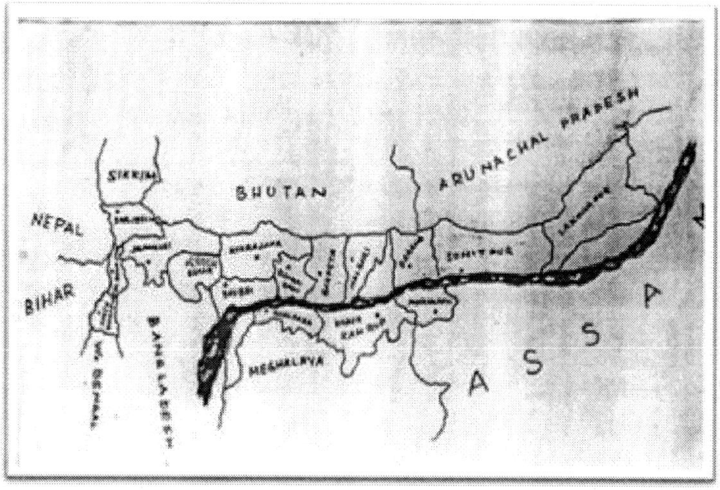

the Lakhya river separates from the Brahmaputra and there it is bounded by the country called Bongo". He further writes that "Kamatapur The King (*Niladhwaj*) having settled his government built a city called Kamatapur (in Cooch Behar) and he and his successors took the title of Kamateswar or Lords of Kamata, while the title of Kamateswary of lady of Kamata, was bestowed on the family deity, a female spirit, as usual, delighting in blood" (Roy:2007:15).

The Rajbanshis identify themselves with the Kamata Kingdom or Kamatapur, Rajbanshi as a political power in this region came much later, almost more than 250 years later; after the Kingdom of Kamata was being established by Sandhya Rai. The Kingdom of Kamata was ruled by different rulers of different dynasties from the period of the mid 13th century to the end of the 15th century.

In most of the writing, Kamatapur has emerged as the capital of the Kamata kingdom. Many times the term Kamata and Kamrup are used synonymously and have been treated as the same kingdom. E. A Gait stated that the western part of the *Brahmaputra valley*, which in the former times, was included in the ancient kingdom of Kamarupa and whose western boundary was the Karatoya; later on it was changed its name from Kamrupa to Kamata. According to him the Muhammadan historians sometimes speak as if the terms Kamrupa and Kamata were synonymous and applicable to one and the same country; but on the other occasions they appear to regard them as distinct, and it would seem that at times the tracts east and west of the Sankosh owed allegiance to different rulers, just as they did in the later days of Rajbanshi rule (Gait: 2011: 42-43).

It is believed that in the year 1260 *Sandhya Rai* shifted his capital from Guwahati to Kamatapur in present-day Cooch Behar to avoid the frequent skirmishers with the neighboring Kacharis and to facilitate the king to effectively engage the invading Muslim rulers from southwestern states. After shifting the capital, it was named Kamta or Kamta-Kamrup and the king adopted the title of 'Kamoteswar' or 'Kameswar'. During this period Kamta-Kamrup kingdom extended its area of control and it has consisted of Cooch Behar, entire Kamrup, Greater Goalpara district of Assam, districts of Mymensingh and Rangpur lying on the eastern side of river Brahmaputra (Roy: 2007: 29).

Sandhya Rai's reign over the Kamrup region came to an end with the rise of '*Bhuiyans*' (large land Lords). Their rule extended from Goalpara to Nagaon in the west and east, from river Brahmaputra to river Subanshiri in the north and river Kopili in the south. One of the most renowned rulers of Kamata was King Durlabh Narayan, who ascended the throne of Kamata in 1330 A.D. to 1350 A.D. and brought all the *Bhuiyans* under his control. Besides the strong administrative arrangement, king Durlabh Naraya took an interest in the development of education, art, and culture. Durlabh Narayan was a great part of learning and his royal count was adorned with many scholars and poet. Most of the ancient books written in *Kamrupi* (or *Kamatapuri*) language ware composed during his region. Under his patronage, the famous poet Hem Saraswati and Harihar Mishra were two great poets who contributed many literary works during his time. Hem Saraswati wrote two important works i.e. '*Prahlad Charit*' and '*Hara-Gauri Sambed*'. '*Laba Kushar Yuddha*' was another such literary work by Harihar Mishra (Roy: 2007: 30). After Durlabh Narayan his son Indra Narayan succeeded the throne from 1350 to 1365. After 1365 Arimatta, the grandson of Dharma Narayan became the king of Kamata and it is believed that he avenged forcible taking over of northern part of Kamata-Kamrup by Durlabh Narayan from his grandfather Dharma Narayan (Roy: 2007: 31). After the take over Arimatta shifted his capital from Kamtapur to Baidyagrah near the river Betna.

In 1440 A. D. a new line of kings emerged in the Kamata region. Niladhwaja was a powerful Kayastha Bhuiyan who became the new king in Kamata who established Khan or Khien Dynasty. The origin of Niladhwaja is not clear but it is believed that due to not getting a proper place in the '*Varna*' system of Hindu caste, Niladhwaja and other Hindu Kayastha kings adopted the title of Muslims as Khan. He was succeeded by his son Chakradhvaj in 1460 A. D. It is said that during the reign of Chakradhvaj, Sultan Barbak invaded the kingdom of Kamata, but was defeated by the former. Chakradhvaj built a temple of the Kaamateswari at Kamtapur. After Chakradhvaj, his son Nilambar took the throne of Kamata (Datta: 2000:70-71). Nilambar was a powerful king among the Khan Dynasty. He extended the kingdom of Kamata from Karatoya in the west to Barnadi in the east of Sonitpur district by annexing the neighboring states. Around 1494 A. D. Nawab Hussain Shah of Gour invaded Kamata and destroyed the capital of Nilambar. Das stated that the downfall of Nilambar was eventually the downfall of the Kamata kingdom founded by Sindhu Rai. It is said that the rise of Koch power within few years after the fall of Nilambar, which changed the history of Kamata in the later years, in the later centuries (Das: 2009: 41).

Now discuss the Khenas and Kamata Kingdon in the early fifteenth century. The Khenas founded a new kingdom in Kamata in the fifteenth century. The Khenas early history and origin are shrouded in mystery. Buchanan Hamilton, during his visits (1807-09) to the ruined sites of Kmatapur Durga, the fortified capital of Kamata Kings at *Gosanimari*, recorded a local tradition about the foundation of the Kamata kingdom by the Khenas. He elaborated that Khenas was a servant of a *Brahmin*, who had founded the Kamata kingdom. The same explained has also given the *Gosani Mangal* (a local Literature), composed by Radhakrishna Das Bairagi the time of Cooch Behar king Harendra Narayan (1783-1839). It elaborated that the story of Kantanath of Gosanimari village, who was a servant of a Brahmin, but he was blessed the goddess *Gosani*. After Kantanath became the king of Kamata, which going through a period of anarchy. He worms the title *Kanteswar*. His one queen Banamala had an extra-marital relationship with Manohar, the state minister's (a Brahmin) son. Kanterswar (the King) being revengeful had killed Manohar and served his cooked meat eat to his father. But the minister (Manohar's father), knowing the atrocious act of the king, he went to take the help of the Sultan of Bengal to destroy Kamatapur (Ahamed: 1990:36-48).

After the destroy of Kamataur, the Tista-Brahmaputra valley become a center stage of the mutual conflict between the tribal and non-tribal landed chiefs due to lack of any central authority. Moreover, local chiefs entitle themselves as King like Rup

Narayan, Mal Kanwar, Ghasa Lakhan, and Lakshmi Narayan, but jointly overthrew Hussain Shahs' control in this region. In such a political situation of Kamata was the Bhuiyans came forward to control the political power. So the Tista-Brahmaputra valley became a sphere of mutual rivalry and lawlessness (Barman: 2007:39).

Among these Bhuniyas one name Hajo turned out is benevolent. He had two daughters Jira and Hira. On the other side in the village of Chiknagram (presently in Kokarajhar district in Assam) was ruled by *Hariya/Haridas Mandal* and the most powerful and took over as headman of the village. The Bhuniyaas Hajo wedded off his daughter to Haridas. In due time Jira gave birth to Madan and Chandan while Hira gave birth to Sishu (*Sisya Singha*) and Bishu (*Biswa Singha*). Among the four brothers Bishu was the braves, cleverest and toughest seriatim these four brothers mastered the art of war and started attacking and winning over the villages surrounding Chikana. Terror spread in holding the neighboring lands. On the run, conflict occurred with Turukh Kotwal of that region. They collected soldiers, elephants, and horses and pulverized upon the Turukh Kotwal. Shisu and Bishu killed many armies of Turukh Kotwal (Kotwal appeared with a big army). But Madan died in this war. Being saddened Bishu along with Sishu attacked severely. Bishu (Biswa Singh) caught the Kotwal's horse and killed the Kotwal.

It was the beginning of *Rajshok* (royal calendar year) in 1510 A. D. Maharaja Chandan was enthroned. After 13 years in 1523 A. D. This region reigned from Biswa Singh. Biswa Singh was crowned next in absence of any son of Maharaja Chandan. And his brother Sisya Singha was entitled as *'Raikat'* or 'Family Guardian' and over his next-generation acquired the Prime Ministerial post. As for his residence, he has given the land of Baikanthapur (present Jalpaiguri district of W.B.). The Raikat Kings of Jalpaiguri were his descendants (Sanyal: 1965:5-8).

According to the historical account, the region of Bishwa Singha's dynasty ruled was some people call as *'Koch Kingdom'*. But most of the Rajbanshi Kings of Bishwa Singha's dynasty used to call it the *'Kamata kingdom'*. The kings never renamed the Kamata kingdom as *'Rajbanshi kingdom'*, *'Koch Kingdom'* or *'Koch Rajya'*, though in the course of time, this kingdom went through various names and lastly was named as Cooch Behar (Koch Bihar) in the colonial period (Das: 2009: 41). It was also noticed that most of the kingdom intended to call themselves as the rulers of the Kamata kingdom. After he took over the reign of Kamata, Bishwa Singha declared himself as Kamateswar (Lord of Kamata). Bishwa Singha's son Naranarayan also declared himself as Kamateswar after ascending the throne of Kamata. Lakhminarayan, king of Koch Bihar (Cooch Behar) declared himself as Kamateswar (Ahamed: 2001:03). According to D. Nath the period beginning from A.D. 1200 to 1500, the Rajbanshis might have maintained their existence with a certain amount of political influence and continued to be so until Biswa Singha firmly established their hegemony in the western Brahmaputra valley in the first quarter of the 16th century (Nath: 1989: 15-16). Though the Rajbanshi Kingdom was there from the 13th century onwards it was only in the 16th century that the Rajbanshis emerged as a strong and influential kingdom. Bishwa Singha a Rajbanshi Chieftain ruled over Kamata from 1515 to 1540 and made the Rajbanshi Kingdom politically very strong.

In the year 1513 A. D. Bishwa Singha ascended the throne of Kamata and declared himself as Kamateswar. There are differences of opinions on the exact year of Bishwa Singh's assumption of power. Some scholars located him in A. D. 1515-1540; some others placed him from A. D. 1509 to 1555. But considering many factors, most of the scholars agreed with the former. Historians believe that after the fateful end of king Nilambar's reign, the kingdom of Kamata started to break up into many fiefdoms under the control of different landlords and as a result, many of them started to declare themselves as kings. Hussain Shah totally destroyed the socio-economic and political structure of the kingdom. As a result, it is believed that at the end of the 15th century therc was anarchy prevailing in the kingdom of Kamata (Roy: 2007: 35). According to N.N. Acharyya:

> "Nawab Hussain Shah of Bengal had attacked and overthrown Nilambar, the last ruler of the Khayen dynasty. The city of Kamatapur was destroyed and a vast area around it was annexed. A colony of Afghans was left in Kamata, who disposed of the local chiefs and took up the civil and military administration under the vice-royalty of Prince Daniel, son of Nawab Hussain Shah. But it did not last long. The local chiefs combined themselves under the leadership of the most powerful of them against the

> Muslim hegemony, and taking advantage of the rainy season, attacked Deniel's garrison and cut it off to the last man. Among these chiefs and their followers by far the most numerous and powerful were the Koches, initially independent of each other, but gradually united under the authority of one among themselves named Bishwa Singha, founder of the Koch Kingdom" (Das: 2009:44).

Mentally as well as physically Bishwa Singha was brilliant with regard to administrative arrangement. After taking over the throne he first conquered the Bhuyans who were much strong at that time. One after another Bishwa Singha attacked and defeated the *Bhuniyas* of *Fulguri, Bijni, Pandu, Rani, Bangaon, Chhaygaon, Barnagar, Beltola,* etc. Gradually he extended his kingdom up to river Karatoya (North Bengal/ Bangladesh) in the west and up to river Barnadi (Sonitpur district in Assam) in the east. He shifted his capital from Sikanagram (present Kokrajhar district of Assam) to Kamatapur (present Cooch Behar district of West Bengal) and declared himself as Bishwa Singha (Kamateswar), the king and his brother Shishwa Singha as prince (Roy: 2007: 38). D. Nath states that after establishing his sovereign power over all petty rulers of the region, Bishwa Singha declared himself as the king. Meanwhile, he had come under Hindu influence and on the day of his formal accession to the throne, Bisu assumed the Hindu name Biswa Singha (Nath: 1989: 26).

After the Biswa Singha of the Biswa Singha's dynasty was king Naranarayan. Naranarayan succeeded his father Biswa Singha and ascended the throne of Kamata. King Naranarayan ruled the Kamata kingdom from A. D. 1540 for about 50 years whose reign could be considered as the most influential and golden period in the history of the *Rajbanshi Empire*. Shukladhwaja alias *'Chilarai'* his younger brother and a brave soldier who was appointed as his Commander-in-Chief to assist the king and commend the state's armed forces. The rest of the brothers were appointed in various capacities to run the state machinery (Roy: 2007: 40). The sovereign power of the kingdom during the reign of king Naranarayan extended to the major part of north-eastern India. H. N. Choudhury observes that at the beginning of this century the Naranarayan conquests comprised "almost the whole of Northern Bengal, Bhutan and Assam as well as the modern States of Kachar, Jayantia, Manipur, Tripura, and extended up to the coast of the Bay of Bengal" (Nath: 1989:75). Besides military glory, king Naranarayn was also interested in the cultural development of the state. J.P. Rajkhowa says that the reign of Naranarayan is important from the point that both Naranarayn and Chilarai were great patronages of learning. His court was delighted with the presence of scholars like *Sankardev, Ram Saraswati, Ananta Kandali, Bakul Kayastha*, and many more. Sankardev composed most of his major works including *Kirtana Ghosa*-sections 1, 17-28, 29, *Rukminir Prem Kalaha, Bhagavata*-Book I, II, IX, XIII, *Rukmini Haran Naat* and others including his last work *Rama Vijaya Naat* during his stay in the Koch Kingdom from 1543 to till his death (Rajkhowa: 2001:44-45) some other valuable literary works patronized by king Naranarayan were Ram Saraswati's *Mahabharat,* Purushottam Bidyabagish (a Pirali Brahmin who worked in the court of Muslim ruler Hussain Shah) Sanskrit grammar *Ratnamala Byakaran* and *Kandali's Bhagawat Gita* (Ray: 2007: 47). Another important contribution of king Naranarayan and his brother Chilarai was their support towards the Neo-Vaishnavite movement by patronizing it. Scholar D. Nath writes of it that "by patronizing the Neo Vaishnavite movement Naranarayan not only made a splendid and lasting contribution to the religious life of North-East but at the same time he served a great social cause, namely that of spreading moral and spiritual education among the masses" (Nath: 1989: 90). After the death of Chilarai at around 1581, the kingdom of Kamata was weakened. The main reason for this was the fragmentation of the Kamata kingdom into two parts between Naranarayan and his nephew and son of Chilarai Raghudeb. Due to the agitation of Raghudeb the kingdom, once the undisputed powerhouse of northeastern India, got divided into two parts, Kamata or Koch Bihar in the west and Koch Kamrup in the east and this gradually lead to weakened the Rajbanshi Kingdom (Roy: 2007: 47).

Following the year 1581, the kingdom of Kamata got divided. The Kamrup went to king Raghudeb and after the death of king Naranarayan, his only son Lakshminarayan ascended the throne of the western kingdom of Koch Bihar (Cooch Behar). King Lakshminarayan ruled over the Kamata kingdom from A.D. 1587 to A.D. 1627. He was a weak ruler as compared to his father Naranarayan. According to D. Nath, "Lakshminarayan inherited very few of the brilliant qualities of his father. Weak and indolent, he was totally unfit to guide the destiny of his kingdom against the imperialistic designs of the

Mughals and the territorial ambition of his cousin Raghudev" (Nath: 1989: 90). Though Lakshminarayan was a weak ruler as compared to his forefathers still the people of North Bengal and Assam always remember him for his contribution towards the *'Vaishnavism'*. In the words of Ahmed, "though Lakshminarayan never had the vision and ability of his forefathers, he still could be remembered by the people of Northeast India, particularly in Assam as one who declared *'Vaishnavism'* as the *Rajdharma* (state religion) of his kingdom" (Ahmed: 2001:151). Moreover, he patronized many more authors, poets and many literary works by them during his period. Govinda Mishra translated Bhagwat *Gita* into the Kamatapuri language during his reign. Madhab Deb who was a chief follower of Sankardev took shelter at Lakshminarayan kingdom after Raghudev the king of Kamrup expelled him from his kingdom. Damodardev was another Vashnavite saint who wrote *Bhakti Ratnavali and Krishna Janma Rahashya* took asylum at Lakshminarayan kingdom (Roy: 2007: 48).

Lakshminarayan passed away in 1627 A.D. at Kamrup. After his death, his son Birnarayan ascended the throne of Kamata. He ruled over the kingdom of Kamata around A.D. 1627 to A. D. 1632. He was a weak ruler as compared to his father. During his rule, the power of the kingdom declined gradually and the king of Bhutan stopped paying the tribute (Choudhury: 1993: 203). Though Birnarayan ruled for a short period he did some considerable work like rebuilding the Baneshwar temple.

Prannarayan was a son of king Birnarayan and ruled over the Kamata kingdom from A.D. 1637 to

A.D. 1665 after the death of his father. A.J. Das states that Prannrayan occupied an important place in the history of the Kamata kingdom as he tried to reoccupy the territories of the undivided Kingdom, which had gone into the hands of the Mughals during the reign of Lakshminarayan. He even occupied Dhaka, the capital of Bengal for a short period while Suja (son of Shajahan), the then Subedar of Bengal was away fighting a battle against Aurangzeb in 1661 (Das: 2009: 50). Prannarayan tried to maintain a good relationship with the neighboring kingdom to ensure the sustainability of his kingdom and to throw away the Mughal power from his kingdom. He also showed his kindness towards religion. In the year 1665, he reconstructed the famous *Kamateswari* Temple at *Gossanimari*. Moreover, he reconstructed many other temples namely, the Baneswar temple, *Sandswar Siva* temple, etc. Prannarayan was also a great patronage of literature and learning. He patronized many scholars like Jaykrisnha Bhattacharya, Kabi Ratna, Srinath Brahman and others who created valuable works like *Proyog Ratnamala, Rajkhandam, Bishwasingha Charitam*, and many more (Choudhury: 1993: 209).

After the death of Prannarayan, his brother Modnarayan took over the throne of Kamata. He ruled over the Koch kingdom from A. D. 1665 to A. D. 1680. Modnarayan was murdered by his relative Jay Narayan and ascended the throne of Kamata. Ray says 'following the incident of the murder of king Modnarayan the internal conflict had begun and the Bhutanese found the time ripe for intervention. The Bhutanese king directly interfered with Koch affairs and the kingdom at Bijni' (Roy: 2007: 53). According to Das "this period, the internal politics of Bishwa

Singha's dynasty became more dramatic and tragic due to the internal conflicts in the royal family, which opened the door for outsiders to interfere in Koch politics. The Bhutanese directly entered into the political arena of the Koch kingdom especially of Cooch Behar and Bijni" (Das: 2009: 51-52).

Modnarayan succeeded his father. From his reign, the influence of Bhutan on Cooch Behar started. He died in 1680 without a male heir. In that situation, Vasudev Narayan, the third son of Prannarayan was placed on the throne. He was killed in a skirmish. Then, Mahindra Narayan, the great-grandson of Prannarayan was placed on the throne. With the death of Mahindra Narayan, Rup Narayan came into power. After a reign of 21 years, he died in 1714. His son, Upendra Narayan remained till 1763. The boy Devendra Narayan was installed as king under the guardianship of Nazir Lalit Narayan. In 1765 Dhairyendra Narayan was placed on the throne, the son of Kharga Narayan (brother of Upendra Narayan). The influence of the Bhutias had increased so much that an office of Bhutan was permanently stationed at Cooch Behar with an army. In later years he was kept in confinement by Bhutan. His son Dharmendra Narayan was installed on the throne. The East Company was watching with concern the growing power of Bhutias close to their borders (Ghosal: 1942:210-283). The appeal for help by Nazir was admitted by the company. On April 5, 1773, the treaty between the young Maharaja Dharmendra Narayan and the East India Company was finalized. Thereafter a peace was concluded between Bhutan and East India Company on April 25, 1774, in consequences of which Dhairyendra Narayan was released from captivity.

Dharmendra Narayan died in 1775 and thereafter Dhairyendra Narayan took over the second time. He died in 1780, leaving his only heir Harendra Narayan. Narendra Narayan succeeded him after his death. In 1859 a topographical survey of Cooch Behar was made by J.G. Pemberton. Nripendra Narayan (one-year-old) succeeded to the throne of his father in 1863. During his minority, the charge of the administration was placed in the hands of a commissioner appointed by the Governor. From that reign, the administration of Cooch Behar entered in Modern phase. The first Commissioner was Colonel J.C.Haughton (Ghosal: 1942:454-469).

The modernization of the administration started by the Commissioners was continued by the Maharaja after the assumption of power. On March 6, 1878, Maharaja Nripendra Narayan was married to Smt. Sunity Devi, daughter of Keshab Chandra Sen, the Brahma reformer (Deb: 2014:187-198). In 1887 the construction of a new palace was completed. The Cooch Behar Palace which is noted for its elegance and grandeur is also protected by the Archaeological Survey of India. This magnificent Palace was constructed by the king Maharaja Nripendra Narayan in 1887 AD. The Palace is fronted by a series of arcaded *verandahs* in the ground and first floors with their piers arranged in an alternate use of single and double rows. The Palace is slightly projected at the south and northern ends and in the center, there is a projected porch to provide an entrance to the Durbar Hall. The elegantly shaped metal dome of the Durbar Hall is topped by a cylindrical louver type ventilator (being 124 feet high from the ground level) recalling the style of the Italian Renaissance. The intrados of the dome is carved in the stepped patterns while the Corinthian columns that support the base of the cupola found a new dimension in variegated colors and designs to an entire surface. The palace comprises various halls and rooms that include the Dressing Room, Bed Room, Drawing Room, Dining Hall, and Billiard hall, Library, Toshakhana, Ladies Gallery and Vestibules. Unfortunately, all the articles and the precious objects as contained by these rooms and halls are now lost and curbed slightly the crowning glory and superb manifestation of the Palace (Deb: 2014:145-148). Maharaja Nripendra Narayan died in 1911 and was succeeded by his eldest son Rajarajendra Narayan. He died in 1913 and was succeeded by his brother Jitendra Narayan. He married Smt. Indira Devi, daughter of Gaekwad of Baroda. He died in 1921 and succeeded by his minor son Jagaddipendra Narayan. He was the last Maharaja of the Cooch Behar.

Figure: -2: Image of Cooch Behar Place (Raj Bari) today the most important tourist sport. Located near the Cooch Behar bus stand.

Maharaja Jagaddipendra Narayan was the eldest son of Maharaja Jitendra Narayan and Indira Devi. He was born on 15th December 1915 A.D. at the Cooch Behar Palace. In his childhood, he took lessons under a home tutor. After that, for higher studies, he was admitted to Hehro in London in 1927. Thereafter he got admitted to Cambridge University in 1929 (Deb: 2016:38).

Maharaja Jagaddipendra Narayan ascended the throne on 6th April 1936 A.D. The state was administered by Regency Council till he attained adulthood (i.e. from 1922 to 1936 A.D.). Rajmata Indira Devi was the President of Regency Council. After ascending the throne Maharaja Jagaddipendra Narayan himself looked after state administration. He was a generous & dutiful king. He took the help of Ministers and Judicial bench in administering the state's proceedings. He was a disciplined king and not an anarchist. Since Maharaja Jagaddipendra Narayan had the mixed blood of the ancient royal family of Cooch Behar and the royal family of Gaikwad of Baroda, he had the inherent qualities of tradition and characteristics of both the royalties. He was fond of his subjects and in order to speculate his subjects' condition used to visit the villages all alone. He fulfilled all aspirations and prayers of his subjects. During his reign, once the state was struck with severe drought. That year he slacked people revenues too much extent. During his time Bengal was starved with natural calamity due to the Second World War in 1940. Thousands of people died of starvation during that time. But while such calamity was yet to strike Cooch Behar at that time, due to good administration under Maharaja Jagaddipendra Narayan there was sufficient supply of food, clothing and other items in the state. At that time Maharaja Jagaddipendra Narayan helped by supplying three lakh Mons (1 Mon=40 Kgs) of rice to Bengal. Maharaja Jagaddipendra Narayan was a good sportsman. He was the captain of the Calcutta Team in the match between the Calcutta Cricket Team and the Indore Cricket Team held in 1943. He was very good in the game of Polo.

Maharaja Jagaddipendra Narayan carried out the state administration through the State Council. He was the President of the State Council. A British Official elected by the Indian Government was the Vice President of that Council. There were different Ministers to look after the Revenue Deptt., Judicial Deptt., Education Deptt., Police Deptt., and Municipal Deptt. The supreme court of appeal was the State Council. Under that, there was the High Court under whom there was Judge Court. The SubDivisional Nayeb Ahilkars used to look after the Dewani and Faujdari cases under the Judge Court. Apart from these the Nayeb Ahilkars also used to look after deed registration, revenue collection, and Civil Supply Department. Supreme Officials of the Municipal, Police, Education & Medical Departments were an Engineer, Police Superintendent, District School Inspector, and Civil Surgeon respectively. Maharaja himself was the Super of the State Military Department which had two branches namely State Infantry and Narayan Guard (Deb: 2014:197-234).

In 1956 Maharaja married Geogina in England. She was a British lady and educated in History at Cambridge University. Maharaja Jagaddipendra Narayan obtained no child.

During Maharaja Jagaddipendra Narayan there was a widespread struggle for Independence in all parts of India. The influence of such movement was also felt in Cooch Behar. In this state, a political organization known as *"Prajamondal"* was campaigning the ideals of the Congress party. Supporters of that organization wanted a merger with the Indian Dominion. Another political party is known as *"Hitasadhani"* was also gaining power. Patrons of that party wanted Cooch Behar to be centrally administered state. Most of the subjects of the land supported that party. Indian Dominion attained independence in 1947. On 20th August 1948 Maharaja Jagaddipendra Narayan in an agreement merged the state with the Dominion Government of India. Thereafter Cooch Behar was transformed into Central Administered State. Maharaja Jagaddipendra Narayan obtained an annual amount of eight lakhs & fifty thousand as his privy purse. Maharaja Jagaddipendra Narayan was left as stateless King. He was deeply felt. Indian Government restored his royalty with due dignity. Even after he was addressed as *"His Highness Maharaja Bhupbahadur"* and treated with the prestigious royal formality.

At last on 11th April 1970, Maharaja Jagaddipendra Narayan breathed his last at Calcutta. Maharaja was shown military honor at the airport. Thousands of people flocked the airport and the royal streets to confer their last reverence to their beloved Maharaja. When his corpse was preceded amidst the flocks of people, his grieved subjects with tearful eyes bade farewell by floral offerings. Thus a 471-year-old kingdom and royalty established by Maharaja Chandan dated back in 1510 A.D. came to an end and the royal sovereignty of Cooch Behar got washed away by Democracy (Deb: 2014:129-132).

Figure: - 3: Cooch Behar state map after Indian Independence Act 7(1)

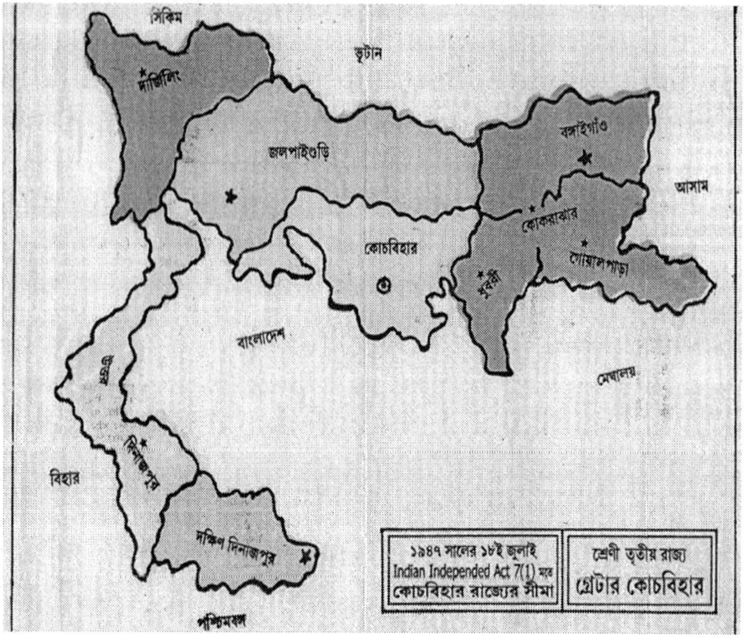

Hitasadhani Dal and Cooch Behar Merger Agreement

The Kamata Cooch Behar state was established by the Kings in the 16th century. During the reign of Nara Narayan, the Kamata Cooch Behar kingdom occupied a vast area of North Bengal and North East India. In the year 1773 by the Anglo-Koch treaty Kochbihar became a tributary state.

Since its foundation, the Cooch Behar kingdom witnessed the struggle between local people (sons of the soil) and the immigrants. Immediately after the accession to the throne, the Rajbanshi kings accepted Hinduism as their religion and Brahmanas were brought by successive Koch rulers from Kanauj, Kasi and other places. But Brahmanism was not accepted by local people. As a result, the king had to allow the local forms of worship prevalent among the Rajbanshi, Rava, Paliya, Koch, Mech and Kachari people. Taking advantage of the Anglo-Koch (Rajbanshi) treaty, John Company began to reorganize the administration of the state according to its own interest and Bengali bureaucrats from South Bengal were appointed as high officials. This policy was disliked and opposed by the native officials. The process of modernization in Cooch Behar culminated after the marriage of Nripendra Narayan with Suniti Devi, daughter of Keshab Chandra Sen in 1878. Henceforth Cooch Behar established direct links with Calcutta and almost all higher administrative posts were occupied by the upper caste Bengalis from lower Bengal. The dominance of the immigrant Bengalis in the administration of the state created a commotion among the local people.

There were other socio-economic causes for the growth of a sense of alienation among the local Rajbansi community of Cooch Behar State. There was no caste system among the Rajbansi community in Cooch Behar. It was the immigrant Bengalis who introduced the practice of the caste system in Cooch Behar. Both jotedars and adhiyars belonged to the same community. Jotedars were at the same time cultivators. With the establishment of British rule, the Rajbansi community was not only alienated from the land and administrative posts but they were treated as Sudras by the immigrant Bengalis. The commotion of the local people culminated against the Bhatias (immigrants from Lower Bengal) with the formation of the Hitasadhani Sabha in 1946. Hitasadhani Sabha was an organization of influential people from among the Rajbanshis (Hindus and Muslims) and other indigenous people. As in other princely states, elections were held in Cooch Behar State. The Hitasadhani Sabha contested the elections and won almost all the seats of the legislative council. This *sabha* (Dal) headed Satish Chandra Roy Singha, the then education minister of Cooch Behar State; vice-presidents Mokhtar Ali Ahamed, the then state inspector of schools and Khan Chowdhury Ahamed, Writer of A History of Cooch Behar, respectively, General Secretary and Board of Director were He manta Kumar Roy Barma (Ahilker) and Kumar Promendra Narayan (Ahilkar) respectively. The post of cashier was in the hands of Md. Makbull Hossain and members were named as Md. Auswer Miah, Jatin Singh; Kamal Krishna Roy Singh (Captain of Hita Sadhani Sabha), Jaladhar Saha, Satish Paul, Harish Chandra Roy Sarkar and others (Das:2005:60). In the elections of 1949, the candidates of Htasadhani Sabha again won almost all the seats. The *Hitasadhani Sabha* received patronage from the influential members of the Cooch Behar Royal family. Most probably Maharaja Jagaddipendra Narayan wanted to retain the princely state status of Cooch Behar within the Indian dominion as per the recommendation of the cabinet mission people. So the Raja patronized Hitasadhani Sabha and also encouraged the fomentation of ethnic sentiments in his own interest.

But the dominance of the local people did not last long. Cooch Behar was merged with the dominion of India in September 1949. After the merger, Cooch Behar became a chief commissioner's province. In the meantime the members of the Hitasadhani Sabha became divided on the question of the fate of Cooch

Behar, one section was in favour of merger of Cooch Behar with Assam, Muslim members of Hitasadhani Sabha wanted that the state should merge with Pakistan and another opinion was that Cooch Behar should remain as a province within the dominion of India. In spite of Nehru's declaration, no plebiscite was held for determining the status of Cooch Behar. It was due to the pressure of Dr. Bidhan Chandra Roy that Cooch Behar was ultimately merged with West Bengal. The Calcutta based middle classes and Bengali intellectuals were desirous to be compensated for the loss of East Bengal due to partition.

Regarding such an issue, the problem of accession was not sustainable. For the integration of the Indian states into a nation, the role of both the Government General of India and His Highness the Maharaja of Cooch Behar is vital to accede in connection with the agreement.

In connection with the finalization of the agreement between the Governor-General of India and His Highness Maharaja of Gooch Behar for the integration of Cooch - Behar State, His Highness raised certain points for clarification; which the Government of India had considered finally and shaped the following arrangements:

(1) It is the intention of the Government of India to the administrator for the present the territories of the Cooch- Behar State as a centrally- administered area under a Chief Commissioner,

(2) All contracts and agreements entered into by Your Highness before the date on which the administration is made over to the Government

of India Will be honored except in so far as any of these contracts or agreements is either repugnant to the provisions of any law made applicable to the State or inconsistent with the general policy of the Government,

(3) The allowances at present drawn by Her Highness the Rajmata will be continued for her lifetime 'and will be paid out of the revenues of the State. You're Highness' brother and other members of the Realing Family will also be paid allowance from the revenues of the States as per list attached,

(4) The responsibility for the Cooch - Behar State Forces will be taken over by the Government of India from 12th September 1949. If these for us as disbanded or any of the men discharged, they will receive the pension or gratuity or compensation, to which they may be entitled under the rules of the States,

(5) Adequate guards will be provided for the protection of Your Highness' person and palace,

(6) No land or building being Your Highness' private property shall be requisitioned or acquired without your consent and without payment of full compensation,

(7) Electricity from the State powerhouse for the main residence of Your Highness and family within the State will be provided at the fixed rate in existence immediately before the transfer of administration to the Government of India. Water supply will be provided free of charge to the main palace of Your Highness and family within the States,

(8) The management of the temples and Debutter properties in the State may be entrusted to a Trust which shall consist of Your Highness as President, three nominees of Your Highness and two nominees of Government. This Trust will be in charge of all temples in the State and will also administer the properties of the temples both inside and outside the State. In the event of the abolition of the zamindaris which are Debutter property, the Government will ensure that the Trust has adequate resources, to fulfill its objectives.

(9) Your Highness may estate a Trust for the marriage of the son and daughter of lsharani of Cooch Behar with a corpus of Rs: 1(one) lakh. The trustees will be beside Your Highness, Their Highness of Jaipur and Dewas Junior,

(10) The civil list of reserve fund of Rs. 10,60,900 shall be Your Highness' Private property and shall· be held by Your Highness in Trust for meeting expenditure in connection with Your' Highness' marriage or special repairs to the Palace and any unforeseen expenditure,

(11) The administration of the Maharaj Kumar Trust fund with a corpus of Rs.4,86,900 shall be formally vested in a Trust of which Your Highness and their Highness of Jaipur and Dewas· Juniog shall be trustees,

(12) Your Highness will be entitled to hold customary Durbars and troops present at the capital viii take part in the Dasserah and other celebration

(13) Your Highness will retain your present ranksn the Indian Army,

(14) The government will Endeavour to associate the name "Narayan" with the Cooch- Behar State Forces· even after their absorption in the Indian Army.

The Ministry of State has issued a Memorandum on the privileges and dignities which have been finalized in consultation with the Rajpramkkhs of Unions and other States. Your Highness will see that the Memorandum deals adequately with the various suggestions made by the Rules from time to time regarding their rights and privileges.

Thereafter, AGREEMENT MADE THIS twenty-eight day of August 1949 between the Governor-General of India and His Highness the Maharaja of Cooch Behar.

Whereas in the best interests of the State of Cooch Behar as well as of the Domination of India it is desirable to provide for the administration of the said State by or under the authority of the Domination Government. (Delatil Agreement on seeing Appendix-B).

In confirmation were of Mr. Vapal Pangunni Menon, Adviser to the Government of India in the Ministry of States has ·appended his signature on behalf and with the authority of the Governor-General of India and Lieutenant Colonel His Highness Maharaja Jagaddipendra Narayan Bhup Bahadur, Maharaja of Cooch Behar has appended his signature on behalf of himself, his heirs and successors.

Table: - 2: As in the original Constitution, 1949 Union (Das Basu: 1980:374)

States in Part A	States in Part B	States in Part C	Territories in Part D
1. Assam 2. Bihar 3. Bombay 4. Madhya Pradesh 5. Madras 6. Orisa 7. Punjab 8. The United Provinces 9. West Bengal	1. Hyderabad 2. Jammu and Kashmir 3. Madhya Bharat 4. Mysore 5. Patiala and East Punjab	1. Ajmer 2. Bhupal 3. Bilaspur 4. **Cooch Behar** 5. Coorg	1. The Andaman and Nicobar Islands 2. Acquired Territories (if any)

Origin of the Statehood Movement

The demand for a separate Greater Cooch Behar state comprising the six districts (*Cooch Behar, Jalpaiguri, Darjeeling, Uttar Dinajpur, Dakshin Dinajpur, and Malda*) of North Bengal for the sons of the soil (Rajbanshis) is not a new movement. The Greater Cooch Behar movement's old identity was Kamatapur movement and the seeds of the demand for a separate Kamatapur state were laid during the merger of princely state Cooch Behar with the Indian Dominion. Cooch Behar was merged with the dominion of Indian on 12th September 1949 and Cooch Behar becomes a chief commissioner's province. Cooch Behar was categorized as 'C' state under an agreement signed by Mr. V. P. Menon, the then advisor to the government of India and highness Maharaja Jagadipendra Narayan, the lost of King Cooch Behar kingdom. On the historic occasion of handing over of power, honorable Home Minister

Sardar Vallabh Bhai Patel sent a message to Sri Najnappa, chief Commissioner of Cooch Behar on the eve of formal handing over function:

> On the Handing over of Cooch Behar to central administration, I sent to its people my best wisher and assurance on behalf of the government of India that though for. Their interest in welfare will claim our close and intimate attention. I am fully aware of the many problems political and economic which affect the state and I am confident that with their cooperation and assistance we would succeed in solving them in the best interest of the state and the country for their happiness and prosperity, unity and mutual adjustment between the constituent elements of the population are essential pre-requisites without this such resources and personnel as we may be able to spare for them would avail little.

The people of Cooch Behar will work with single mildness and devotion to duty as a united team for their own betterment and achieve their due place in the political and administrative setup of Indian.

But unfortunately on 19th January 1950, Cooch Behar was merged with the province of West Bengal which an 'A' category state. The merger with West Bengal did not satisfy the sons of the soil of Cooch Behar. As a result, the Rajbanshis Claim the separate state and emerging the statehood movement in Cooch Behar (North Bengal) and demand separate state Kamatapur or Greater Cooch Behar state. The Leaders of the *Greater Cooch Behar* Movement believe that if Cooch Behar is made a 'C' category state, their political aspiration will be fulfilled and all-round development of the region will be possible. Thus the merger of Cooch Behar with West Bengal is illegal, their demand.

Being deprived socio-economically the Rajbanshi people become marginalized in North Bengal and were losing their identity, culture, and language in their homeland where once the rulers and the ruled belonged to the same ethnic group. Out of such grievances, the Uttar Khand Dal was formed on 21 June 1969. Initially, they put forward an 18-point-charter a demand to redress the grievances of the people of North Bengal. Having failed to get a response from the West Bengal government the *Uttar Khand Dal* demanded a separate Kamatapur state comprising six districts of North Bengal on 10 March 1971. To extend its mass base *Uttar Khand Dal* Clearly stated that it was not a party of any one ethnic group but was a part of all those who lived in North Bengal. Immediately after the formation of Uttar Khand Dal a new student organization named Uttar Banga Tapashilee Jati O Adivasi Student Organization was formed in 1977 to look after the interest of the subaltern students. It was due to the movements of this student organization that North Bengal University was compelled to introduce reservation system for SC/ST students in 1977. The UKD failed to extend its mass base because the poor, local people were not as yet disillusioned with the Left Front Government and were especially affected by its pro-people slogan.

Afterward, the *Kamtapur People's Party* was formed in 1996 under the leadership of Atul Roy. Apart from the demand for separate statehood and recognition of the Kamtapuri language, the KPP demanded the expulsion of illegal foreigners from North Bengal as per the Indira-Mujib accord of 1971. In support of their ten-point-demand, KPP organized a cycle rally, blocked the National Highway and on 6th June 1998 called a 24 hour North Bengal Bandh. However, due to internal dissension KPP was divided into two factions led by Nikhil Roy and Atul Roy. This division weakened the KPP movement. During this period emerged the Kamtapur Liberation Organisation, an extremist outfit. KLO had links with ULFA (United Liberation Front of Assam).

Figure: -4: One time the leaders of the movement demand below area (Map)

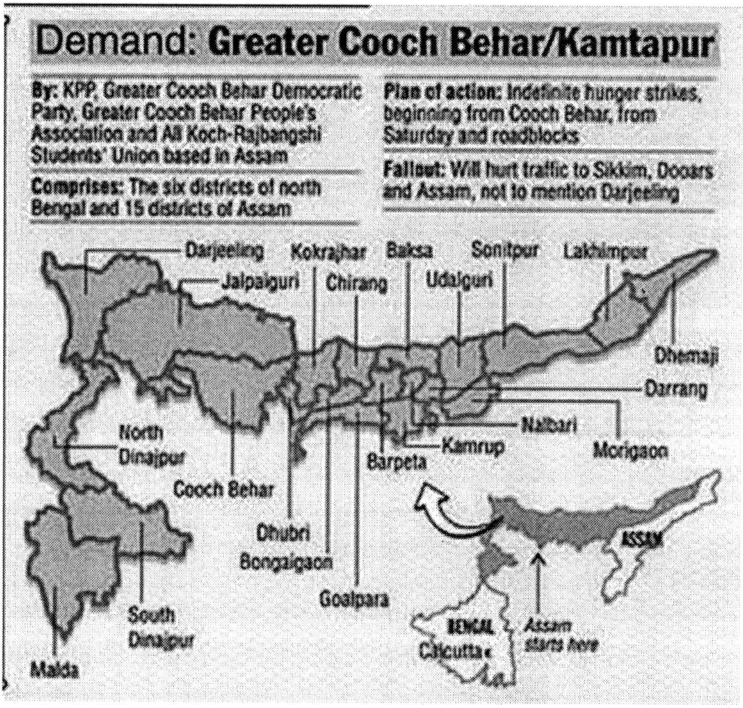

Recently the Greater Cooch Behar movement has emerged which has raised a legal question on the merger of Cooch Behar with West Bengal. The main demand of the Greater Cooch Behar movement is that Cooch Behar is declared a 'C' category state and placed under a chief commissioner's administration. The movement claims Cooch Behar was merged with West Bengal without taking the consent of the people. The greater Cooch Behar people's association submitted a memorandum to the president of India, the prime minister and the home minister on 26th December 2000 for declaring Cooch Behar a 'C' category state and forming a caretaker ministry for Cooch Behar. In support of their demand, the movement organized mass gatherings, hunger strikes, etc. Later on, due to internal squabbles, the Association was divided into two groups, namely the greater Cooch Behar people's association and the Greater Cooch Behar Democratic party. In a bid to strengthen their movement for a separate state, the greater Cooch Behar Democratic party, *Kamtapur progressive party* and Assam's *All Koch Rajbanshi Students' Union* formed a greater Kamta joint forum at Dinhata demanding the formation of a bigger Cooch Behar state. Their demand is to form a state with 4 districts of Assam, 6 districts of North Bengal and two districts of Bihar. Their demand is for an area almost the same as it was in the heyday of the Kamta-Koch Kingdom in the 16th century.

Figure: -5: Image of demand homeland of movement members.

REFERENCES

Acharya, N. N. (1996), *A Brief History of Assam: From earliest time to the year 1983*, Omsons Publications, Guwahati.

Adhikary, Harikishore (1314 BS), *Rajbanshi Kula Pradeep (Bengali)*, Calcutta.

Ahamed, Kha Chowdhari Amanatulla (1990), *Cooch Beharer Itihas* (Bengali), Modern Book Agency Pvt. Ltd., Kolkata.

Barma, Sukhbilash (2004), *Indian Folk Music Bhawaiya Ethnomusicological study*, Global Vision Publishing House, New Delhi.

Barman, Rup Kumar (2007), *Contested Regionalism: A New Look on the History, Cultural Change and Regionalism of North Bengal and Lower Assam*, Abhijeet Publications, Delhi.

Barman, Upendra Nath (1941), *Rajbanshi Kshatriya Jatir Itihas* (Bengali), Jalpaiguri.

Basu, Durga Das (1980), *Introduction to The Constitution of India* (eight editions), Prentice Hall of India Pvt. Ltd., New Delhi.

Basu, Swaraj (2003), *Dynamics of a Caste Movement: The Rajbansis of North Bengal 1910-1947*, Manohar Publication, New Delhi.

Berevly, H. (1872), *Census Report of Bengal*, Vol.- I.

Bhamaritantra, 2nd stanza.

Chowdhury, H. N. (1903), *Cooch Behar State and its Land Revenue Settlement*, State Book Press, Cooch Behar.

Census of India (1921). Net link: http://www.censusindia.gov.in/census_and_you/old_report/censu-1921.aspx. Access on 20 January 2017.

Dalton, E.T. (1872), *Descriptive Ethnology of Bengal*, Office of the Superintendent of Government Printing, Calcutta.

Das, Arup Jyoti (2009), *Kamatapur and the Koch Rajbanshi Imagination*, Arunima Deka Publication, Guwahati.

Das, Dhirendra Nath (2005), *Regional Movements, Ethnicity and Politics*, Abhijeet Publications, Delhi.

Das, Sukumar (1982), *Uttarbanger Itihas (Bengali)*, Kumar Sahitya Prokashan, Kolkata.

Data, D. (2013), *King Nara Narayana's Military Campaigning in North-East India: An Analysis Through Numismatics*, The NEHU Journal, Vol. XI, No. 1. PP-35-43.

Deb, Ranajit (2014), *Cooch Behar Zelar Itihas (Bengali)*, Purbottar Prokashan, Cooch Behar.

Deb, Saswati (2016), *Cooch Beharer Raj Kahini-O-Rajprasad*, Tribitta Prokashan, Cooch Behar.

Gait, E.A. (2011), *A History of Assam*, Guwahati, Spectrum Publication, Delhi.

Ghosal, Sarat Chandra (1942), *A History of Cooch Behar*, Cooch Behar State Press, Cooch Behar.

Hadgson, B. H. (1949), *On the Origin Location, Numbers, Creed, Customs, Character and Condition of Koch, Bodo and Dhimal People; with General description of the climate they dwell*, in Journal of Asiatic Society of Bengal, Vol. XVIII, Part.- II.

Hamilton, Buchanon (1810), *Account of the District of Rangpur*, Appendix- III of the District Census Handbook, Jalpaiguri and Cooch Behar, West Bengal, 1915.

Hunter, Dr. W.W. (1876), *A Statistical Account of Bengal*, Vol. X, Concept Publishing Company, New Delhi.

Majumder, R.C. (2011), *History of Bengal*, Vol. I. BR Publishing Corporation, Delhi.

Nath, D. (1989), *History of Koch Kingdom*, Mittal Publication, New Delhi.

O'Malley, L. S. S. (1911), *Census Report of India*, Vol- V, Part- I(Bengal).

Porter, A. E. (1931), *Census of India*, Vol- V, Part- I.

Rajkhowa, J. P. (2001), *Generalissimo Chilarai and His Times*, Vikram Publishers, Guwahati.

Roy, Manomohan (1902), Some Notes on the Rajbanshi, *Journal of Asiatic Society of Bengal*, Kolkata, Vol- LXXI, No.- 2.

Roy, Nalini Ranjan (2007), *Koch Kingdom and Kamatapur: the Truth Unveiled*, Vicky Publication, Guwahati.

Risley, H.H. (1891), *The Tribes and Castes of Bengal*, Vol-I, Bengal Secretariat Press, Calcutta.

Sanyal, Charu Chandra (1965), *The Rajbansis of North Bengal*, The Asiatic Society, Kolkata.

Siungha, Khetra Nath (2011), *Rai Saheb Panchanan Barmar Jiboni (Bengali*), Dr. Nripendranatth Pal (ed.), Anima Prakashani, Kolkata.

Tarkaratna, Panchanan (1384 BS), *Kalika Purana*, Nababharat Publishers, Kolkata.

Thomson, W. H. (1921), *Census Report of India*, Vol- V, Part- I (Bengal).

Waddle, L. A. (1975), *Tribes of the Brahmaputra Valley*, Read Books, Delhi.

2

Panchanan Barma and Rajbanshi People

Panchanan Barma also popularly known as Takur Panchanan and Rai Saheb was a Rajbanshi leader and reformer for the Rajbanshi society of North-Eastern India during the period of British rule in India. He was the Father of the Rajbanshi community of undivided state Cooch Behar (Barman: 2015:35). Panchanan Barma sacrifices his life for his community. He had taken many reformations works for the recover the lost dignity of the Rajbanshi Society. He was shocked by contemporary social discrimination and economic inequality. Zamindars and moneylenders had crippled the rural economy by rampant exploitation. The only reason for their backwardness is low education as well as unconsciousness about society. Panchanan Barma established a *'Kshatriya Samiti'* in 1910 to help the Rajbanshi peoples and local community to develop their condition. This Samiti was involved in social activities works for this community (Barman: 1401 BS: 29-32)

Rai Saheb Panchanan Barma, the Rajbanshi Kshatriya leader was a leading figure in the social atlas of the twentieth century North Bengal and part of North East India. His activities were not only confined to the Rajbanshi community but also touched the heart and soul of the people of Goalpara and Assam. He was the most remarkable personality of the social campus and a pioneer social reformer, political activities and a man who identified himself with the peasants of the community. Panchanan Barma was a man who gave a new life to the majority of the people of Cooch Behar, Rangpur, Jalpaiguri, Dinajpur (both North and South) and lower Assam.

Birth, Education, and Walks of Life:

Panchanan Barma's birth name was Panchanan Sarkar. He was born on 11 February 1866 at Khalisamari village, Mathabhanga Sub-division, in erstwhile Cooch Behar State. His father's name was Mr. Khoshal Sarkar and mother's name was Mrs. Champala Sarkar (Singha: 2004:6-8). Khoshal Sarkar was a rich respectable landlord man and renowned *muktean* in the court of Mathabhanga.

Educationally the Rajbanshis were backward. They lacked the zeal towards education and therefore the educated Rajbanshis were rare. The half-educated Rajbanshis could neither work in the field as a farmer nor could live a respectable life in learned society. The condition of the Rajbanshis was worse.

The primary education of Panchanan Sarkar took place in a nearby village pathshala. After primary education, Khosal Sarkar being an encouraging father admitted his son in Mathabhanga Middle English School which was about six miles from Khalisamari. Panchanan's intellect and passion for learning gave him success in the M. E. Examination which is evident from the Cooch Behar Gazetteer (Adhikary: 2014: xviii-xix).

Before going to the brief sketch of the academic life of Panchanan it is necessary to note that he grew up from a state which was quite pessimistic towards education and from an illiterate society to achieve the first lesson of education. However, after his M.E. Examination Panchanan was admitted to Jenkin's School and having stood first in the Middle English School in the Rajshahi Division he did not require to pay fees of the School for four years as he was awarded the Medal Scholarship of the Government of Rs. 4/- per month.

He graduated from a Kolkata college, with honours in Sanskrit, in 1893. He later privately completed his M. A. in Mental and Moral philosophy in 1896 from the University of Calcutta, and later took his L.L.B. Degree from the Ripon College, Kolkata in 1900 (Barman:1379B.S.:8). In the early years of his career, he started practicing law at Rangpur court, in Rangpur. He was shocked by the refusal of a high caste lawyer to use a toga (lawyer's gown), previously used by him. In the following years, he led a *Kshatriyazation* movement among the Rajbanshi community of Bengal. In order to be respected and accepted by the upper caste Bengalis Panchanan felt the Rajbanshis must get organized and educated, which he tired to achieve thought the *Kshatriya Samiti*. Understandably, the Samiti tried to prove that Rajbanshis were kshatriyas with a royal lineage, suggesting a historical link with Bhaskarvarman, the king of Kamarupa. Based on Sanskrit literature and Brahmin pundits, they also claimed to be *Kshatriyas*, hiding their true identity for centuries. In support of this claim, the movement involved a ceremonial kshatriyaization process - brahminical rituals were performed to convert thousands of Rajbanshis to 'Kshatriya Rajbanshi' in the villages of North Bengal (Singh: 2011:49-52). In 1921, Panchanan was selected to the Bengal Legislative Assembly after winning the general election. Panchanan Barma's died in Kolkata on 9th September 1935.

Figure:-6: Image of Manishi Panchanan Barma (1866-1935).

Panchanan Barma and Kshatriya movement

In India, it is generally around religion that the caste system, which is principally a custom-based structure of social hierarchy, has grown up. It is linked with the unequal distribution of power and wealth also. In essence, the caste system is a consequence of the socio-economic and political process rooted in history. One of the most remarkable features was, 'The constant rivalry between various communities for political and economic power which was reflected in their varying and conflicting perceptions of Brahmins and the Vedas' (Gupta: 2000:194). On the other hand the British, in order to prolong their rule, lent some credibility to the caste system in the administrative sphere. That is why Dirks says, "Under colonialism caste became a specifically Indian form of civil society, the most critical site for the textualization of social identity, but also for the specification of public and private domain, the rights and responsibilities of the colonial state, the legitimatization consisting of social freedom and social control, and the developments of the documentation and certification regimes of the bureaucratic state (Bosu: 2003:13-14).

The caste system became important in India in the cultural sphere on one hand, and similarly in the social, politico-economic and administrative spheres on the other. Because just as the feudal structure did not collapse with the fall of the *Mughal Empire*, its later transformation into a subservient political and economic entity in the colonial period is a historic event. In consequence, caste-based movements emerged in British India. It may be mentioned that such movements in different parts of India were *anti-Brahminical* in nature. In North Bengal and North-Eastern India, the Brahminical domination was absent, but other problems cropped up. It was against this background that the 'Kshatriya movement' led by Panchanan Barma was a remarkable phenomenon. This movement assumed the shape of a social mass upheaval in today's North Bengal, and in North-Eastern India as a whole. Panchanan Barma gave able leadership to this movement. For this reason, Swaraj Basu has remarked, "Panchanan Barma was the main ideologue of the Movement" (Bosu: 2003:88).

The English too was active in perpetuating the Indian caste-based social stratification. This gave rise to various problems in Indian society. On the other hand, various communities of different parts of India were trying to find ways of coming out of these problems. The *Kshatriya* movement led by Panchanan Barma was the outcome of such a reaction. It was also one kind of Renaissance. The Renaissance came to Bengal mainly in the fin-de siècle decades of the eighteenth century and continued well into the nineteenth century. A good number of books and numerous articles have been written in various personages, who belonged to the first half of the nineteenth century. While searching for facts about them, it has been found difficult to accept many of the then prevalent notions. Hence it is not unjustified to throw light on Panchanan Barma's social thoughts on the basis of newer facts. In truth, the concept of Renaissance is such that it can be applied to any culture and any phase of history (Samaddar: 1985:4).

The origin of the caste movement among the Rajbanshis could be located in the ill-treatment and humiliation meted out by the upper caste Hindus. Census Authority in 1891 gave instruction to the effect that the Rajbanshis is the same as Koch and as such the Rajbanshis Kshatriyas be returned with the Koch community as had done in the previous census of 1872. The *Kshatriya* movement against the census authority had started under the leadership of Sri Haromohan Roy a local *zamindar* of Shyampur (Rangpur) who lived Rajbanshis Kshatriya by caste.

He had also formed a samiti called *"Rangpur Vitya Kshatriya Bidhayani Sabha"* for the Rajbasnshi of Rangpur with the view to improve the conditions of his Community.

On 10th February 1891, a protest letter was lodged with the District magistrate F.A. Skyne urging him to recognize Rajbanshi as a separate caste from the Koch and also allow them to enroll as in the census. The District Magistrate sought the opinion of Rangpur Dharma Sabha which was the mouthpiece of Hindu religion and an association of Pundits. The Dharma Sabha called a meeting as the convention on 15th March 1891. It was attended by more than 400 representatives of *Pundits Samaj* of Hindu religion and after a long discussion, it was concluded that the Rajbanshis of North Bengal hat *Kshatriya* descent and Hindus. The *Rajbanshis Kshatriya* had fallen as degraded from the Kshatriya position because of the non-observance of Vedic rites and rituals and should be considered as Vratya Kshatriya. The decision of the convention was conveyed to the District Magistrate on the 18th March 1891. Accepting the opinion of the convention the District Magistrate F.A. Skyne made a strong recommendation on April 3, 1891, to the Superintendent of Census to permit the Rajbanshis to be enrolled a Vratya Kshatriya against the Caste status. On the 18th of May 1891, he issued a circular that from 1 Jaistha 1298 B.S. Rajbanshis may write themselves as Vratya Kshatriya in official papers and matters. All the efforts of the Rajbanshi leaders and movement had not returned any results and the recommendation of F.A Skyne in 1891 was not accepted. Again in 1901, the Kshatriya movement gained momentum (Bosu: 2003:100-101).

Then Panchanan Barma felt the need for legal assistance in the bid to secure justice for the Rajbanshis Community. Census Report of 1901, Buchanan Hamilton suggested, "all Rajbanshis are not Koch, but most of them are." This leads to the easy inference that Koch and Rajbanshis are two different communities. But Rajbanshis Community fills they are separate for Koch. Panchanan Barma proved it that Koch and Rajbanshi are separate castes. Panchanan Barma established *"kshatriya Samiti"* on 1st May 1910 in the theatre hall of Rangpur and he adorned this chair all along with his life (Barman: 1379 BS: 08).

In the year 1317 BS (1910 AD) is the most remarkable year in the life of Panchanan Barma. In the third conference of Uttar Banga Sahitya Sammelan held in Gouripur town on 9 and 10 Magh,1316, Panchanan presented the article on *'Kamta Bihari Literature'* which was published in the minutes of the Sammelan in 1317 B.S. And on Baisakh 18, 1317 (May 1, 1910) was established the *Kshatriya Samiti*. Haramohan Khajanchi, the zamindar of the Shyampur area of Rangpur district and the architect of *'Rangpur Bratya Kshatriya Jatir Unnati Bidhayani Sabha'* expired in the meantime (Dey: 1420 BS: 137-139). The *Samiti* was origin mainly at the initiative and management of Panchanan, a resident of Coochbehar and a young lawyer, a newcomer to Rangpur. Although regeneration of the Rajbanshi Kshatriya community was the main objective of organizing the *Kshatriya Samiti,* it was not improbable that there were at least two reasons associated with the event. The first and foremost reason was the non-availability of a suitable job in his birthplace, Cooch Behar then under feudal rule. Whether due to the opposition put up by the caste

Hindu officials in the higher up or due to the aversion of the then Maharaja Nripendra Narayan to get directly involved in the matter of employment of the highly educated son of the soil Panchanan, the fact remains that Panchanan did not get a good job in Cooch Behar and as such he had to desert his own place to earn honorable livelihood with his head high. He has already had the taste of caste-list hate and negligence of caste Hindus for the Rajbanshis even after he started practicing law (Dey: 1420 BS: 135-145).

In the year 1913 under the leadership of Panchanan Barma, Rajbansis held a great union (*mahamilan)* festival in Parulbari village (P.S. Debigunj) on the bank of the Karatowa River. On the eve of the festival, Panchanan Barma said that "we (Rajbashi) are *Kshatriya,* and *Kshatriya sons and daughters.*" Here it should be mentioned that in 1910, at the time of the formation of the Kshatriya Samiti, many wanted to retain the word Kshatriya only. But Panchanan Barma's stand was unequivocal, "If the term 'Rajbanshi' is dropped, our mission will be defeated (*hamra hareya jamo*)." In a word, it can be argued that the decision, taken by Panchanan Barma, to build up the Rajbansi Kshatriya identity through the Kshatriya movement was a historic one. Moreover, it was due to the protest of the Kshatriya community led by Panchanan Barma that in the report published by Malley, the then Census Superintendent it was said that Rajbansis and Koches are two different identities (Barman: 1401 BS: 80). In north Bengal also the Rajbanshiwere found to have passed through at least three distinct identities in different censuses – from Rajbanshi to Bratra Kshatriya (census in 1891) Vadra Kshatriya to Kshatriya Rajbanshi in census 1911, 1921 and Kshatriya Rajbanshi to Kshatriya in census 1931 (Choudhury: 2013:01).

Women Empowerment and Education:

The worth of a civilization can be judged by the place given to women in society. One of several factors that justify the greatness of India's ancient culture is the honorable place granted to women. The Muslim influence on India caused considerable deterioration in the status of women. They were deprived of their rights to equality with men. Raja Ram Mohan Roy started a movement against this inequality and subjugation. The contact of Indian culture with that of the British also brought improvement in the status of women by their imperial policy (Das: 2013:470). The third factor in the revival of women's position was the influence of Mahatma Gandhi who induced women to participate in the Freedom Movement. But in the contemporary of North-eastern India Panchanan Barma actively exellerated the Women empower among *"The Naari Raksha Committee"*. As a result of this retrieval of freedom, women in Indian have distinguished themselves as teachers, nurses, air-hostesses, booking clerks, receptionists, and doctors. They are also participating in politics and administration. But in spite of this amelioration in the status of women, the evils of illiteracy, dowry, ignorance, and economic slavery would have to be fully removed in order to give them their rightful place in Indian society.

Women in present-day society wives and mothers and working women-are ready to accept an inferior position in the family, society, and polity. They were at the forefront and active participants in the social and economic life of the county. Their status was reduced to a lower level and were treated inferior to men. Due to this, the social and economic situation of the nation also deteriorated. But Social reformation in the nineteenth century by the light of renaissance women's society of Bengal had been benefited. By the nineteenth century, Rammohan and Vidyasagar had shown their interest to grow to empower among women through women-education and activities of social reforms, like them, Panchanan Barma played the same role for the women in the first half of 20th century Bengal. The mainstream of the social reform movement in the 19th century was to develop the social statue of women (Sengupta: 1999:15). According to Panchanan Barma, both men and women are of equal rank, but they are not identical. They are peerless pairs, being supplementary to one another, each helping the other so that without the one the existence of the other cannot be conceived. The concept of self is the most important factor affecting the behavior of women. The self-realization of the potential of women was severely restricted in the pre-independence period due to various socio-cultural conditions and conditioning. Panchanan Barma stressed women's participation in political, socio-cultural and economic spheres through his various political and social activities. He argued that the cultural empowerment of women can be a reality only when women are treated on par with men, through all the differences that are part and parcel of being a different gender. There should be a change in the mindset of society on a fundamental level. Above all, women's economic participation and empowerment are fundamental to strengthening women's rights and enabling women to have control over their lives and exert influence in society. It is about creating just and equitable societies. It is true that women often face discrimination and persistent gender inequalities, with some women experiencing multiple discrimination and exclusion because of factors such as ethnicity or caste.

One focal point of Panchanan Barma's activities was the spread of modern education, particularly that of women's education. He wanted to lift the women folk from the utterly humiliating and degrading conditions and to establish them on the foundation of their own rights. During 1921-23, abduction and rape of women assumed menacing proportions in the Rangpur region. In 1923, a lady named Barada Sundari was forcibly abducted and raped. Then a number of ladies, namely Tadhamani Barmani, Gritakumari Baishnabi, Kanduri Barmani, etc., were raped one by one. Against such oppression, Panchanan Barma raised the voice of protest. He built up an organization named *Nari Rakhsa Samiti* (Committee for the Protection of Women). Through this organization, he sought to make women self-reliant by giving them proper education and by training them in stick-play, sword-fight and wrestling. He did not receive any cooperation from English rulers, yet he persisted in his work. If this fact is taken into account, it will perhaps not be far out of truth to argue that Panchanan's success far exceeded that of Rammohan and Vidyasagar. It was Panchanan who first, in a debate in the Bengal Legislative Council in 1921, spoke of women's franchise. Here the thrust of his argument was, "Our conception is not that the house is a house but that it is the women in the house who is really the house."

That is why the Panchanan Barma wanted to view women's freedom as not simply a case of politics (Barman: 2015:10-11). At present, we come across a large number of discussions about women's freedom and rights but are it possible to establish this freedom and right unless society becomes civilized and conscious. Women's freedom lies in the relation of mutual respect between men and women, and Panchanan's perception of this truth can be detected in his poem 'Dangdhari Mao'. In this poem, Panchanan Barma exhorted the youth community to stand up against wrongs and injustices. At that point in time, it acted like a tonic.

Rural Development and Kshatriya Bank

As far as the ideas on rural development are concerned, Panchanan Barma has a specific similarity with Rabindranath Tagore, although Tagore preferred the term rural reconstruction to rural development. His opinion was that there was a collective strength in the villages, which had enabled the villages to sustain themselves for more than 2500 years. In order to use this strength effectively, Tagore advocated the formation of cooperatives or groups.

Under the leadership of Panchanan Barma, well-coordinated clusters of villages (gram mandali) grew up in Rangpur, and the number of such clusters exceeded 300. The Kshatriya Bank's impact on these clusters was very much discernible. Here too one can find a similarity between Tagore and Panchanan Barma. In Tagore's opinion, there was no alternative to the release of the energy of villager's latent in them, and that all the villages of the country were to be reconstructed in such a way that they would be able to meet all their needs (Barman: 2015:714).

In fact, economic reform formed one of the more remarkable reformist activities of Panchanan Barma. He set up a concern named Barma Company that operated within the region now known as Bangladesh. The real objective of the Company was to free the rural poor peasants from the exploitation by landowners and moneylenders. The most remarkable of Panchanan Barma's economic reform activities was the formation of *'Khastriya Bank'*. In the areas then predominantly inhabited by Rajbansis, a change was noticeable. The people of the Rajbanshi community were trying to shift from the mainstream of their traditional economic system (Bosu: 2003:51-52). Panchanan Barma understood that no social upliftment of the community was possible unless the community could be economically strengthened, and hence he set up the Khastriya Bank in the Bengali year 1327 (Singha: 2004:6-8).

In order to understand the nature of the functioning of this bank, it is necessary to have some knowledge of the banking system in greater Bengal. The sense in which the word 'bank' is used was absent in the pre-Plessey period. In the eighteenth century, the bank's functions were divided into three categories: - (a) the acceptance of deposits from the public. In those days, wealthy persons used to deposit their money in banks in lieu of interest. (b) Give short and long-term loans at interest. (c) To issue various types of hundis (bills of exchange) and realize their values, and to participate in the sale and purchase of imported and exported goods. Along with these, banks used to take part in the exchange of coins. In the pre-Plassey period, the House of Jagat Seth was the foremost banking institution of Bengal. The House of Jagat Seth was connected with deposit banking and credit banking, but they did not issue notes. This house may be compared with Germany's 'Phutzer' and Holland's 'Trip' families (Mukhopadyaya: 2001:148).

Being a rural person by birth and early upbringing, he was familiar with the economic conditions of the countryside. While living in Rangpur, he began to reflect on how to improve the lot of the peasantry and to bring prosperity to the village-centered economy. The changes brought about by the English-instituted land revenue system were not at all beneficial to the villages. This system gave rise to changes that did great harm to the rural people. The creativity of the villages was hampered, and they were made dependent on the outside world. The high rates of revenue extraction rendered the villagers helpless and destitute. To liberate them from this condition, Panchanan Barma set up the 'Kshatriya Bank'. Its objective was to free the peasantry from the clutches of the landowners and moneylenders and to provide them with the opportunity to build up a bright future by providing them with easy credit facilities. The new method he applied is today called micro-finance, but earlier known as micro-credit. This micro-credit system conducted through the Kshatriya Bank benefited many peasants. But he also understood that provision of easy credit through the Kshatriya Bank would not be enough to free the peasantry from usurious exploitation. For this reason, he sought to establish the rights of peasants through land reform laws (Panchyataraj Patrika: 2011:16).

Panchanan Barma was a compassionate man for farmers. He made a general fund to help poor farmers. Those poor peasants were given financial help on behalf of the Kshatriya Samiti led by Panchanan Barman. The main objective to establish the *Kshatriya Samiti* is to protect farmers from exploitation by the landlords and moneylenders. He founded 'Barma Company for the financial help of the poor peasants. The company was not able to provide financial support to each farmer so he established the Kshatriya bank led by Kshatriya Samiti at Rangpur. The farmers were given loans from the bank in easy terms and conditions. As a result, poor farmers were released from the huge loan of money lenders. After actively involved in politics, he attempted to correct the Bengal Tenancy Act for farmers. After the pressure of Panchanan, the Government made an amendment draft and passed the Tenancy Act in 1885. Panchanan Barma was a member of the said committee. Earlier, the peasants had no ownership of the land. *Zamindars* were converted their name on the land instead of farmers by pressure. Burma Panchanon arranged land ownership to farmers. As a result, poor farmers had benefited.

By the year 1930-31 when the World economic crisis raised in most of the countries, then Bengal farmers became landless by the tyranny of *Zamindars* and *traders*. In the meantime, members of the Assembly were requested to the Government to protect the farmers and a land searching committee was formed. Thus, 'The Board of Economic Enquiry' was formed. Panchanan Barma was a member of the board. He announced the Moratorium in order to protect farmers from ruin. As a result, The Bengal Money Leder Act was passed in 1934. Panchanan played an important role to pass the law. He makes provision for the Bengal Agricultural Debtor's Act and as an immediate effect, most of the peasants were benefited (Adhikary: 2014:104-114).

This chapter lastly may say that Panchanan Barma's *Kshatriya* Reform Movement has pushed forward his society to a greater extent of prestige and social status in caste-based Bengal as well as India. Panchanan Barma has been able to prove that the Rajbanshis were Kshatriya from the earliest period of time. Universality and diversity is a unique characteristic of India. Peoples of several castes and creed, religion and belief, live here peacefully maintaining one's own individuality. So Panchanan, for his Rajbanshi society as well as for all, tried to develop culture and tradition. The Indian economy is based on villages. So he tried to develop villages with economic reformation by the scheme of micro-credit or microfinance. For making proper use of money with the help of Banks he established 'Kshatriya Bank'. Thus he wanted to form a strong country self-reliant and self-confident one. For this purpose, he wanted to form co-operative groups. A woman is an important half of a man. With any development of one half, another half can't be developed. So Panchanan Barma did much for women's emancipation and empowerment.

REFERENCES

Adhikary, Madhab Chandra (2014), *Rajbanshi Samaj O Manishi Panchanan Barma (Bengali)*, Reader Service, Kolkata.

Barman, Kartick Chandra (2015), *Social Reforms Activities of Manishi Panchanan Barma towards Rajbanshi Society: A Brief Historical Perspective*, North Asian International Research Journal of Social Science and Humanities, NAISRJC, Vol.-1, Issue-2.

Barman, Kartick Chandra (2015), *Social Philosophy of Manishi Panchanan Barma: A Brief Study on Historical Perspectives*, IJARIIE, Vol-1, Issue- 4.

Barman, Kartick Chandra (2015), *Economics Thought of Panchanan Barma and Kshatriya Bank: A Brief on Historical Perspective*, Historical Research, Science Publishing Group.

Barman, Upendra Nath (1401 BS), *Kshatriya Jatir Itihas*, Jalpaiguri.

Barman, Upendra Nath (1379 BS), *Thakur Panchanan Barmar Jibon Charit*, Jalpaiguri.

Basu, Swaraj (2003), *Dynamics of a Caste Movement: The Rajbansis of North Bengal, 1910-1947*, Manohar Publication, New Delhi.

Choudhuri, Arjun (2013), *Koch and Rajbanshi: Confusion or Fusion*, Net link: https://www.kochrajbanshicentre.org/2013/09/16/Koch_and_rajbansi_confusion_or_fusion. Access on 15 January 2017.

Das, Pran Gobinda (2013) *Bharatio Rastro Chinta O Jatio Andolon*. NCBA, Kolkata.

Dey, Andhendu Mouli (1420 BS), *Rai Saheb Panchana Barmar Kshatriya Andolon (Bengali)*, in Goswami, Kamalesh (ed.), Bidrpoha-O-Andolane Uttarbanga, Priya Book House, Kolkata.

Gupta, Dipankar (2000), *Interrogating Caste: Understanding Hierarchy and difference in Indian Society*, Penguin Publication, New Delhi.

Mukhopadyaya, Subodh Kumar (2001), *Economic History of Bengal*, Kolkata.

Panchayat Raj Patrika 2016.

Samaddar, Ranabir (1985), *Bharater Jatio Andolon O Jatio Sanghatir Samasyad (Bengali)*, West Bengal State Book, Kolkata.

Sengupta, Dr. Gitashree Bandhana (1999), *Spondita Antarlik*, progreesive publication, Kolkata.

Singha, Kshetra Nath (2004), *Rai Saheb Panchanan Barmar Jibani (Bengali)*, Dr. Nripendra Nath Pal (ed.), Anima Prakashani, Kolkata.

3

Objectives of the Greater Cooch Behar Movement and Its Future

There are a peculiar character and distinction of the demand for a separate state by the Rajbanshis and also other ethnic communities of India. In Northeast India when demand for a separate homeland comes from a particular community, the proposed homeland is generally named after that particular community. Like the Bodo Community is demanding *Bodoland*, the Nagas are demanding *Nagalim*, the Dimasas are demanding Dimaraji, Gorkha's demand is for Gorkhaland, etc. But interestingly Rajbanshis are not demanding *'Kochland'*, or *'Rajbanshiland'*. They are not using the ethnic name for their proposed separate state. Rajbanshis are demanding *Greater Cooch Behar (Kamatapur)* as a separate state which is rooted in the historical memory of their erstwhile Kamatapur Kingdom. Therefore, to understand the present Greater Cooch Behar movement the Rajbanshis, it is important to know the nature of historical memory of the Kamatapur Kingdom which was established by Sandhya Rai in the mid 13th century comprising areas of present-day Assam, North Bengal, and Bangladesh.

The autonomy movement by the Rajbanshis seeks the creation of a separate Kamatapur state comprising the same areas of present North Bengal and Assam under the constitutional provision. The movement also looks for the recognition of Kamatapuri or Rajbanshi language under the Eight Scheduled of the constitution of India along with the demands of cultural and socio-economic development of their community. In the case of Assam, the movement also demands Scheduled Tribe status for the Rajbanshis living in North Bengal. Presently, many organizations are spearheading the demand for the separate Greater Cooch Behar state. Two organizations are of considerable importance among those. The Kamatapur Peoples' Party (KPP) Greater Cooch Behar Peoples' in North Bengal and All Koch Rajbanshi Student's Union (AKRSU) in Assam have been quite active since their inception. At the same time, Kamatapur Liberation Organization (KLO) a militant organization formed in 1995 is working in support of the demand for a sovereign Kamatapur state. They are demanding the establishment of a separate state for the Rajbanshis living in the northern parts of West Bengal and the Western part of Assam. All Kamatapur Students' Organization (AKSO), a new student organization, has joined recently in the movement for the separate Kamatapur (Greater Cooch Behar) state. Greater Cooch Behar People's Association is a strong movement in North Bengal based organization agitating for the creation of a separate state of 'Greater Cooch Behar' (Barman: 2007:119-121).

Figure:-6: Image of AKRSUs processional for separate state Kamatapur (Greater Cooch Behar) in Assam

Subsequently, there are some other non-governmental and literary organizations of Rajbanshis which are working for the socio-cultural development of their community with sympathy to the demand for autonomy. *'The Koch Rajbanshi Sahitya Sabha'* of Assam and 'Kamata Sahitya Parishad' in North Bengal are two literary organizations working on the area of language, culture and literary works of Rajbanshis. Similarly, there are many literary organizations based in Assam, North Bengal, Bihar, Meghalaya, and Nepal that are working on the socio-cultural and literary issues of the Rajbanshis. Recently, under the leadership of Vijoy Chandra Barman 'Rajbanshi Vasa Akademi' has started to work for the development of Rajbanshi language in North Bengal. 'Rajbanshi Cultural Society'

is another Assam based literary organization working for the development of Rajbanshi's history, culture and literature along with the territorial demand.

Name of some major Socio-political organizations which demand of Separate Greater Cooch Behar (Kamatapur) state (table no. 3):

Table: - 3

Sl. No.	*Name of the Organization*	*Nature*	*Place of origin*	*Foundation Year*	*Original Aim*
1.	Hitasadhini Dal	Political	North Bengal	1949	Separate State
2.	Uttar Khanda Dal	Political	North Bengal	1969	Separate state
3.	Uttar Banga Tapashili Jati O Adibashi Sangathan	Social	North Bengal	1969	Social change
4.	Kamata Rajya Dabee Parishad	Political	Assam	1969	Separate state
5.	Koch-Rajbanshi International	Social/ Political	Assam	1984	Separate state
6.	Kamatapur Gana Parishad	Political	North Bengal	1985	Separate state
7.	Bharatiya Kamata Rajya Parishad	Political	Assam	1986	Separate state
8.	Kamatapur Liberation Organization	Political	North Bengal	1993	Separate state
9.	All Koch Rajbanshi Student Union	Political	Assam	1993	Separate state
10.	Kamatapur Peoples Party	Political	North Bengal	1995	Separate state
11.	All Kamatapur Student Union	Political	North Bengal	1987	Separate state
12.	Uttar Banga Rajya Sangram Parishad	Political	North Bengal	1996	Separate state
13.	Greater Cooch Behar Peoples' Association	Political	North Bengal	1998	Separate state
14.	All Kamatapur Student Organization	Political	Assam	2004	Separate state
15.	Kamatapur Association	Political	Assam	2010	Separate state

16.	Chilarai Sena	Military	Assam	2014	Separate state
17.	Narayani Sena	Military	North Bengal	2014	Separate state

Sources: Rup Kumar Barman's book *Contested Regionalism* and another some books.

I below discuss the most important three organizations' objectives/demands of the Greater Cooch Behar movement in West Bengal. So are UKD, KPP, and GCPA.

Uttar Khanda Dal

On 5th July 1969, the UKD was formed at the historical Jalpesh temple of Maynaguri of Jalpaiguri district with Panchanan Mallik, Kalindra Nath Barman, Hiramohan Barman, Soma Oraon, Sitanath Roy and many others and they demand separate state Kamatapur (present Greater Cooch Behar) in order to protect the people of North Bengal from the exploitation of 'Calcutta-Centric capitalist leaders'. This movement's also popularly known as the Uttarkhand movement. The objective of the UKD was the setting a part of the region of North Bengal and the creation of a separate state called Kamatapur state for protecting the people of North Bengal from the exploitation of South Bengal. The Party (UKD) assured that in their proposed new state the people would reside peacefully irrespective of caste, class, and creed (Ray: 2007:111-131). The nature, character, and content of the movement, its strategies and objectives have undergone a series of changes with the change in the leadership styles and method.

The Uttarkhand movement led by the UKD in early 1970 started peacefully through public meetings covering the villages of North Bengal. However, it was in only in the 1980s that the UKD made a general call for a separate state for North Bengal the Kamatapur state and they send a letter/application Indian Prime Minister Smt. Indira Gandhi in March 1981. It gave wide publicity to the concept of statehood through various leaflets, p[amphlets, manifestos and public meetings under the leadership of Panchanan Mallik, Sampad Ray, and others. The Dal comes forward with a charter of demands that included, among others,

- Formation of Kamatapur state consisting of five districts of North Bengal.
- Reservation of 80% of jobs of central, state and other semi-government for the sons of the soil.
- Introduction of Kamatapuri as the medium of education up to the school level.
- Broadcasting of news and other program relating to agriculture, music, drama and other cultural functions in Kamatapuri language on all the radio stations of North Bengal.
- Reservation of 80% of recruits from North Bengal in defense services for the sons of the soil, setting up recruitment boards in each district and relaxation of age and height of *Rajbanshi, Rava, and Mech* candidates.
- Following the *Indra-Mujib* agreement, 1971, should be the base for Citizenship.
- Reservation of seats for the residents of North Bengal in the university of North Bengal, North Bengal Medical College, Jalpaiguri Engineering college and Cooch Behar Agriculture College.

- No handing over of the Tin Bigha of Cooch Behar to Bangladesh.
- Exchange of Chit Mahal of India and Bangladesh.
- Setting up of High Court in North Bengal etc.

Figure: - 8: Map's of UKD demand area

Kamatapur Peoples' Party

The Kamatapur Peoples' party (KPP) formed under the leadership Atul Roy in 1995 was an offshoot of the UKD. The party demanding the formation of a Kamatapur state comprising six districts of North Bengal (Cooch Behar, Darjeeling, Jalpaiguri, Malda, North and South Dinajpur). The formation of KPP has marginalized virtually all other organizations to their call for the creation of a separate state of Kamatapur (presently Greater Cooch Behar). The KPP apart from the six districts of North Bengal has also demanded Goalpara, Dhubri and Kokrarjhar District of Assam and KPP were many demands (seen Appendix-C and Appendix- D).

The KPP argues that the region is the original homeland of the Kamatapuries i.e. predominantly *Rajbanshis, Khens, Meches, Koibatyas* and that there is a constant marginalization of the Kamatapuris by the intruders, there is a need for the creation of the state of KJamatapur for the KAmatapuris. The basic arguments are that the Kamatapuris constitute 70% of the total population of North Bengal and culturally, linguistically, socially and historically different from that of Bengalis. The KPP argues that Kamatapuris are economically backward and the situation of Kamatapuris is responsible for the Government of West Bengal's irresponsible. KPP argues that the dignity socio-cultural identity and economic interest of the local people would be protected only with the creation of a separate state for Kamatapur.

The Kamatapur movement which has seen an upsurge in the *Cooch Behar, Jalpaiguri, Darjeeling, Malda, North, and South Dinajpur (North Bengal)* of West Bengal is an ultimate outcome of the struggle for power and the associated privileges between the sons' of soil (particularly the Rajbanshi) and the Bengali (Das: 2007:137-164). The main argument is that the North Bengal region originally belongs to the Kamatapuri who are predominantly Rajbanshis in terms of caste and are culturally, linguistically, socially and historically distinct from Bengalis. It argues that the Kamatapuris though 70% of the total population of North Bengal, have lost their identity because of the continuous influx of Bengalis or Bhatias from Bangaladesh (Jana: 2008:153-195).

The Kamatapur movement under the KPP and its leadership is a well-organized movement compared to that of UKD and other associations which had demanded Kamatapur. There several organizations that operate and mobilize support for the movement. These organizations included the AKSU, KVSP, the Intellectual Front, and the Kamatapur Women's rights Forum which is the women's front. The most militant and controversial of the organization is the KLO.

In the year 2006 Atul Roy, in turn, broke away from KPP and origin a new party as *Kamatapur Progressive Party*. However, the objective of both the functions was similar as both the parties were primarily concerned with mobilizing support for the creation of a separate state of Kamatapur.

The Greater Cooch Behar People's Organization

The Greater Cooch Behar People Association was founded on 9th September 1998 (*23th Vadar, 1405*) at the Premise of Kakribari Primary School under the President Ship of Kumar Anilendra Narayan, Nearest Brother of Maharaja Jagadipendra Narayan Bhupbahadur and General Secretary Arun Kumar Roy by the grace of Sri Ananta Ray. The GCPAs' main aim to fulfill the Treaty on 28th August 1949 in between Govt. of India and His Highness of Maharaja Sri Jagadipendra Narayan Bhup Bahadur, the then king of Cooch Behar Princely State. This Association aims to form Cooch Behar 'C' Camp State in Indian

Constitution adopted on 26th November 1949. It also aims to establish Political administration in the Greater Cooch Behar State (Debnath: 2016:110-117). As per as the Treaty GCPA aims to develop Language, traditional Culture, Literature, History, Ancient heritage, Communal Harmony, Economical Growth, Religious, Social awareness, Geographical infrastructure of the People of Greater Cooch Behar State and thereby exclusive development for all kinds of People of the Cooch Behar Princely State irrespective of Cast and Creed will be Possible. The GCPA's basic objectives are to (details have been given in Appendix-E to Appendix-F).

- Maintain the cultural heritage of Cooch Behar,
- Take steps to solve the problems of Cooch Behar,
- Safeguard the interest of the Cooch Behar people,
- Improve the living and social condition of the people of Cooch Behar,
- Promote the unity, fraternity, and cooperation among the Cooch Behar people,
- Take steps for maintaining the clause of the merger agreement made between his Highness Maharaja of Cooch Behar and the union of India.
- Give the status of Cooch Behar as Class 'C' State as was mentioned at the time of the merger of Cooch Behar State with Union of India (Barman: 2007:136).

Presently The Greater Cooch Behar People Associations movement is a highlight position in West Bengal. This organization member was many strategies to fulfill their demand (i.e. *huger, strike,* etc.) over 5000 in number from the Cooch Bihar region of West Bengal have been on hunger strike – without food and water– for the past three days demanding a separate state. Trains filled with these ethnic bonafide *Rajbanshi* people flocked to the national capital to press their demand for Cooch Behar within the Union of India, carved out of the 10 districts of West Bengal and Assam. In the past two days, as many as 80 protesters have been claimed to be hospitalized due to weakness resulting from the *Bhookh Hartal* (hunger strike) (Uttarbanga Sambad:2005:01). One person, in fact, swooned in front of this author, who was at once rushed to the hospital. Nirmal Roy, the President of *the Greater Cooch Behar People's Association, to* understand the issue. Roy tells us that like other princely states, His *Highness* of Maharaja ruled Cooch Behar joined the Union of India by signing the instrument of accession with the latter on August 28, 1949. Later, Cooch Behar was placed as 'C' Camp State in the Indian Constitution adopted on November 26, 1949. "But on January 1, 1950, our constitutional Cooch Behar state was amalgamated with the 'A' Category state of West Bengal by dint of '290 A' British provincial Act of 1935 by Governor-General. But this Act was fully abandoned in 1939 during World War II by the British and was not in existence in 1950. Therefore, the merger of Cooch Behar 'C' camp state with the 'A' category state of West Bengal was completely illegal and unconstitutional. Roy claims five districts of Cooch Behar, namely *South Dinajpur, North Dinajpur, Darjeeling, Jalpaiguri, and Cooch Behar* were merged with West Bengal while other five districts – *Kokrajhar, Chirang, Bongaigaon, Dhubri, and Goalpara* – went with Assam.

Figure: - 9: some images of GCPA members and supporters
Hunger strike in 2005

On 21st February 2016, the movement for the greater Cooch Behar was revived this week after almost a decade with a massive mobilization of supporters on the railway tracks at New Cooch Behar railway station. The agitation was called off after police swung into action after 72 hours and the shocking death of three railway passengers, stranded in stalled trains for hours. Police have taken into custody at least 15 leaders of the *Greater Cooch People's Association (GCPA)* who had been spearheading the agitation demanding Union Territory status for Cooch Behar district. But the top leadership – headed by Bangshi Badan Barman — seems to have either gone underground or is in the 'protective custody' of the security forces. The sudden momentum for the Greater Cooch Behar movement and the delayed response of the West Bengal state police and the railway administration in dealing with the blockade are to be viewed in the backdrop of the upcoming state assembly elections in April-May. The leader of the present agitation Bangshi Badan Barman went to jail after an ugly flare-up in 2005 for the greater Cooch Behar statehood movement (Uttar Banga Sambad:2016:01). Five people were killed in Cooch Behar town in clashes between GCPA supporters and the police. The dead had three policemen including an additional superintendent of police. In jail since September 2005, the Mamata Banerjee government classified Bangshi Badan and his 40-plus other associates as 'political prisoners' and they were freed in 2015. Cooch Behar rarely enters newsrooms in Delhi or even, for that matter, Kolkata. The *Rail Roko* in February 2015, though, was an exception. Led by Bangshi Badan Barman from the *Greater Cooch Behar People's Association*, the protest demanded a Cooch Behar state, carved out of West Bengal, Assam and in some of the most imaginative versions even Rangpur district in northern Bangladesh as a home for the Rajbanshi people of the area. Here, far away from the heartland of Bengal, a statehood agitation is brewing, pushed by the region's native population, the Rajbanshi people. The movement has long been suppressed by Kolkata often violently and has even been accused of violence itself. While the police reaction might differ, like the Jat reservation demands, the Bharatiya Janata Party seems to be sympathetic to Rajbanshi statehood. The BJP has allied with sections of the Greater Cooch Behar People's Association to fight the 2016 West Bengal Assembly elections. As a minnow, unable to break into the Bengali mainland, the BJP is trying to chip away at the state's edges, supporting ethnic movements with grouses against Kolkata. The largest of these is the Gorkhaland movement in Darjeeling and the BJP is trying to replicate that model with the Rajbanshi people. But the 2016 West Bengal Assembly election has breathed some fresh air into its sails, with the Bharatiya Janata Party allying with the Greater Cooch Behar People's Association, a party whose principal demand is the creation of a state for the Rajbanshi people. Presently this movement growing up successful because the BJP supports this movement and the BJP now Central Government in India.

Figure: - 10: Images GCPA's 4-day rails stroked in New Cooch Behar Station

নিউ কোচবিহার
न्यू कौचबिहार
NEW COOCH BEHAR

ANI

Future of Greater Cooch Behar Movement

In the following section, an attempt will be made to analyze and interpret the data collected during the field visit. The prime objective of the study was to examine the socio-political movements led by the Rajbanshis to negotiate their various crises. With this objective field studies were conducted during the month of January and February 2017 and data were collected through a semi-structured interview schedule comprising twenty questions (nine-question for interviewers personal and eleven questions for topic-related). Interview both personal and group has been taken from the members of different socio-political organizations of Koch Rajbanshis i.e. local people, local politicians, members of legislature assembly, *member of Panchyat, All Koch Rajbanshi Students Union* (Assam), *Kamatapur Peoples Party* and *Greater Cooch Behar Peoples' Associations* members. To know the opinion of Rajbanshi

Figure: -11: Images after four-day police force baton and kadan gas on the rails striker GCPA members.

peoples the district of Cooch Behar. It is generally felt that only a section of the population will have a piece of extensive knowledge about the problem of the Rajbanshi related to their many issues, therefore the study has applied purposive and snowball sampling for selecting the respondents. The sample size was a hundred (100). There is no specific area has been selected for the study but most of the study was conducted in the Northern part of West Bengal. The data collected from the field survey are analyzed and interpreted below.

In order to study the nature of consciousness of the Rajbanshis about their linguistic and how they see their own language, one question was asked to the selected respondents. They were asked to linguistics the language that they would like to talk about in their social life. Three options were given to the respondents, *Kamatapuri/Kamrupi*, Bengali, and others.

In response to the question relating to the linguistic that they would like to talk in their social life, as shown in the table below (Table-4), 58 percent of the respondents talk that Kamatapuri/Kamrupi is their language. 42 percent as Bengali and 0 percent of the respondents opined that none of the above-mentioned identity they would like to consider in their social life. They select the answer from the options as others. This question highlights a point that some people talk to Kamatapuri local language but they respond to Bengali.

Table- 4: Tabular representation of the Respondents opinion to the question relating to language that they would like to talk in their social life

The language that They Would Like to Talk	*No. of Respondents*	*Percentage*
Kamatapuri/Kamrupi	58	58
Bengali	42	42
Others	0	0
Total	**100**	**100**

In fact, it was observed that most of the people were aware of the fact that they speak Kamatapuri Rajbanshi language and their identity is Rajbanshi. From the last two decades especially from the 1990s, there is a growing tendency of identity consciousness among the Rajbanshis and in this regards many socio-cultural and literary organizations have been playing a crucial role. Greater Cooch Behar Peoples' organization was formed in the year 1998. They play a crucial role in creating awareness among the common masses for their identity-related issues. It was observed among most of the Rajbanshis that now they are more conscious about their glorious past history, about their culture, tradition, etc and are trying to revive their food habits, traditional dress, literature, music to name a few.

Figure-12: Bar Diagram showing the Opinion of the Respondents to the Question relating to linguistic that they would like to talk the language in their Social Life (in percent)

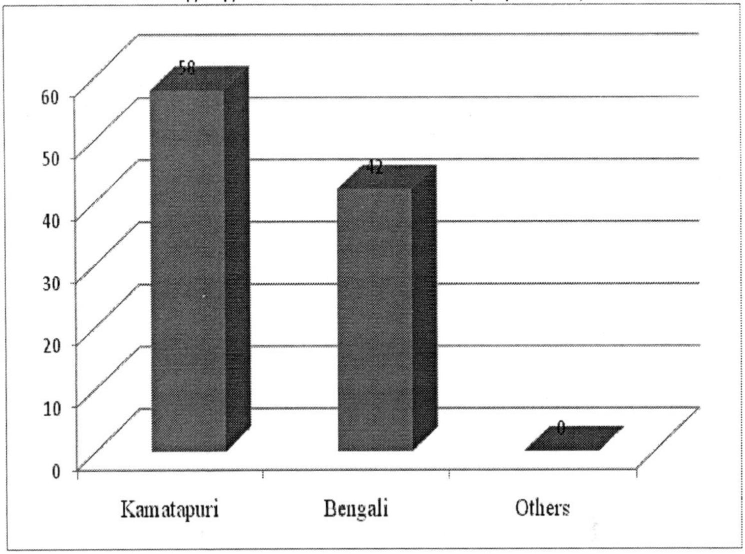

In order to assess the perception of the respondents regarding the support base one question of the Greater Cooch Behar movement. 75 percent of Rajbanshi people answer they have supported this movement. 25 percent of people answer they do not support this movement.

Table-5: Tabular representation of the Respondents opinion to the question relating support base of the movement

Support this movement	*No. Respondents*	*Percentage*
Yes	75	75
No	25	25
Total	**100**	**100**

Figure- 13: Images Thousands of people in the present of GCPA assembly

Figure-14: Pie Diagram showing the Opinion of the Respondents to the supported population of this movement

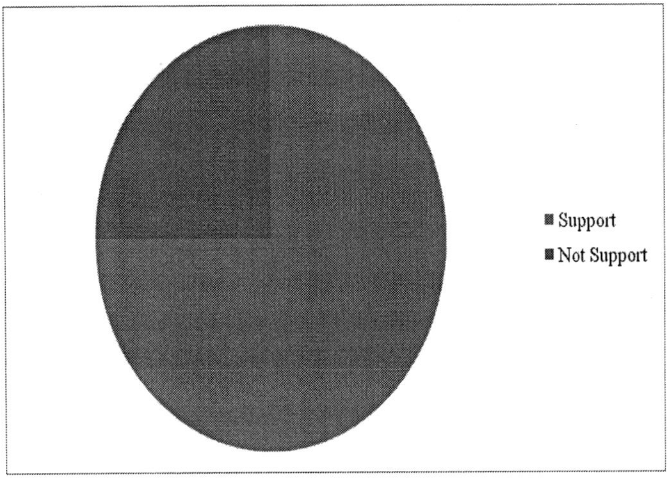

After the supported question, I indicated question respondents of direct involvement the movement or indirectly involved the movement in the response. Here 25 percent of people say that there are directly involved in the movement (they are a member of the organization statehood movement). 50 percent of people say they have indirectly involved this movement (only support the movement not member any organization) and 25 percent people say that they are do not involved and dislike the separate statehood movement (no response).

Table- 6: Tabular represent of Respondent, involved the movement

The response of involved movement	*No. of Respondents*	*Percentage*
Direct involved	25	25
Indirect involved	50	50
No response	25	25
Total	100	100

The above data highlight the majority person supports the movement. But the movement does not succeed a long time because only directly involved persons conducted the movement and indirectly involved people are only mentally or ideologically support the movement, they are no involved any work this movement. They only mentally support the movement of outside.

Figure- 15: Bar Diagram showing the Respondents opinion involved in the movement

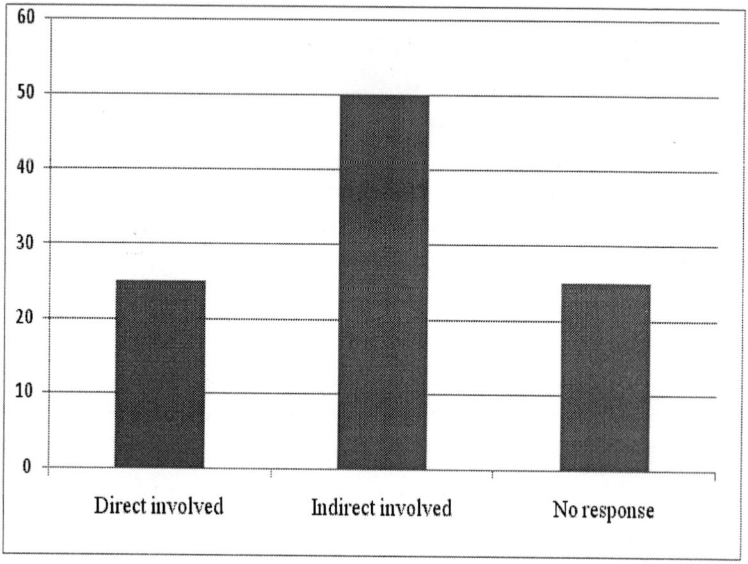

In order to assess the perception of the respondents regarding the Rajbanshi Community and other community support base of the Greater Cooch Behar movement one question was posed to the respondents. The response was varying as shown in the table below (Table-7). Fifty-seven (57) percent of the respondents opined that the Greater Cooch Behar movement was supported only by the Rajbanshis. Forty (40) percent of the respondent opined that this movement supported other communities besides the Rajbanshi, they are local people son of the soil. 3 percent of the respondents opined that the Greater Cooch Behar movements who are supported don't know.

Table-7: Tabular representation of respondents' opinion regarding the support base of the Greater Cooch Behar movement

The support base of the Greater Cooch Behar movement	*No. of respondents*	*Percentage*
Only Rajbanshis	57	57
Others Peoples	40	40
Don't know	3	3
Total	100	100

Figure-16: Bar Diagram showing the Respondent's Opinion regarding the Support base of the Greater Cooch Behar movement (in percent)

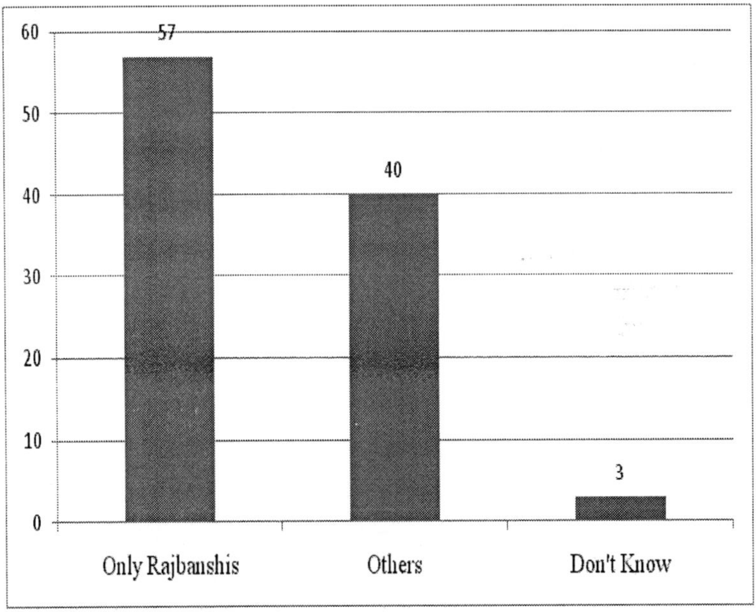

It was observed from the responses of the respondents that the Rajbanshis want Greater Cooch Behar at any cost and all the members of their community support it. It is important to emphasize that many respondents felt that all the local people sons of soil living in the Rajbanshi dominated areas are support the demand of Kamatapur to accept the Bhatiya community (who are come for Purbo Bango and Western Bengal).

To know the opinion of the respondents as regards to state government response towards the Greater Cooch Behar movement a question was asked to the respondents. The respondents were asked to identify whether the government response was positive, negative or partially positive. In response to the question as shown in the table below (Table-), twenty (20) percent of the respondents felt that the government response was positive. Forty-seven (47) percent of the respondents opined that the response of the government was negative and thirty-three (33) percent of the respondents opined that the response of the government was partially positive.

Table-8: Tabular representation of Respondent's Opinion regarding the state government response towards the Greater Cooch Behar movement

State government response towards the Greater Cooch Behar movement	*No. of respondents*	*Percentage*
Positive	20	20
Negative	47	47
Partially positive	33	33
Total	100	100

Figure-17: Pie Diagram showing the Respondents' Opinion regarding the state government response towards the Greater Cooch Behar movement

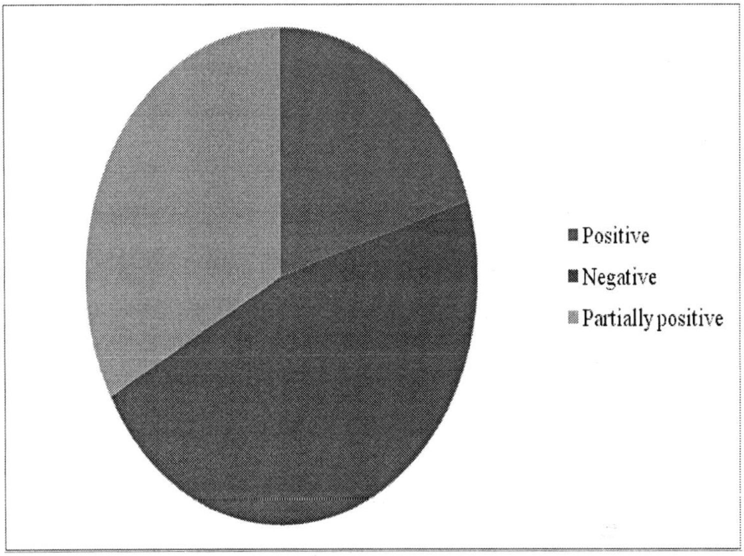

The above diagram show state government does not support the movement but presently the TMC government many offer and activity on this community development. For example, the TMC government processing the Kamatapuri Rajbanshi language enlisted in seven Tapasil in the Constitution of India (*Uttar Banga Sambad:* 2017:11).

Another of the opinion of the same question of the respondents as regards to central government's response towards the Greater Cooch Behar movement was asked to the respondents. Here respondents (table) seventy-eight (78) percent felt that the central government response was positive. Five (5) percent of the respondents felt that the response of the central government was negative and seventeen (17) percent felt the response of the central government was partially positive.

Table-9: Tabular representation of Respondents' Opinion regarding the central government response towards the Greater Cooch Behar movement

Central government response towards the Greater Cooch Behar movement	*No. of respondents*	*Percentage*
Positive	78	78
Negative	5	5
Partially positive	17	17
Total	100	100

Figure-18: Bar Diagram showing the Respondents' Opinion regarding the central government response towards the Greater Cooch Behar movement

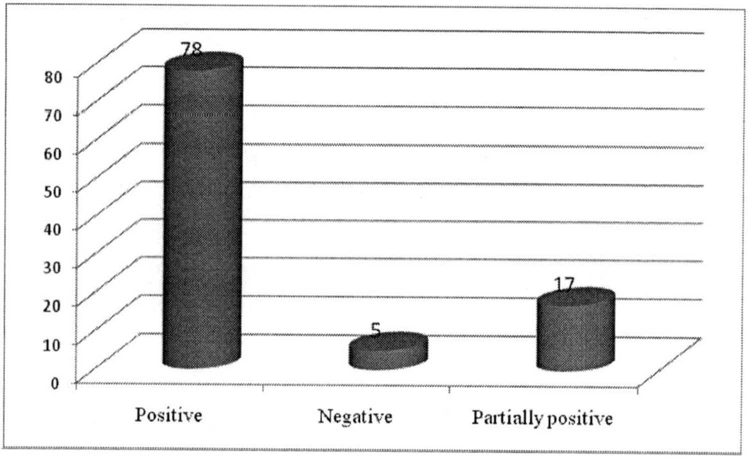

Here above two diagram (figure- and figure-) show a different view for state and central government. It is true. Some examples of the Central government activity on this movement i.e. Narayani Sena training for BSF (Ananda Bazar Patrika: 2016:06), join assembly for BJP and GCPA, etc.

Figure:19: Some images of BJP leaders and GCPA leaders in join Assembly

In order to assess the perception of the respondents as regards the possible causes behind the Greater Cooch Behar movement, respondents were asked to choose from six options to identify the causes responsible for the Greater Cooch Behar movement. In response to the question, the respondents gave different views as shown in table no.10. Seventeen (17) percent of the respondents opined that the ethnic identity crisis of the Rajbanshis. One (1) percent of the respondents considered the wrong policies of the government. Three (3) percent of respondents believed that the Greater Cooch Behar movement was a result of the impact of modern civilization. Similarly, ten (10) percent of the respondents considered undeveloped were an important factor for the Greater Cooch Behar Movement while fifteen (15) percent considered that the Greater Cooch Behar Movement origin's main causes were Cooch Behar Merger in West Bengal 1950. However, a majority of fifty-five (55) percent of respondents opined all the above-mentioned factors (i.e. ethnic identity crisis, land wrong policies of the government, the impact of modern civilization, undeveloped and merger in West Bengal) as responsible for the Greater Cooch Behar movement. They felt the Greater Cooch Behar movement was the result of a combination of all the above-mentioned factors.

Table-10: Tabular representation of Respondents' Opinion as regards to the causes responsible for the Greater Cooch Behar movement

Causes responsible for the Greater Cooch Behar Movement	*No. of respondents*	*Percentage*
The ethnic identity crisis of the Rajbanshis	17	17
Wrong policies of the government	1	1
Impact of modern civilization	2	2
Undeveloped	10	10
Cooch Behar merger in West Bengal in 1950	15	15
All the above	55	55
Total	100	100

Figure-20: Bar Diagram showing the Respondents' Opinion regarding the causes responsible for the Greater Cooch Behar movement

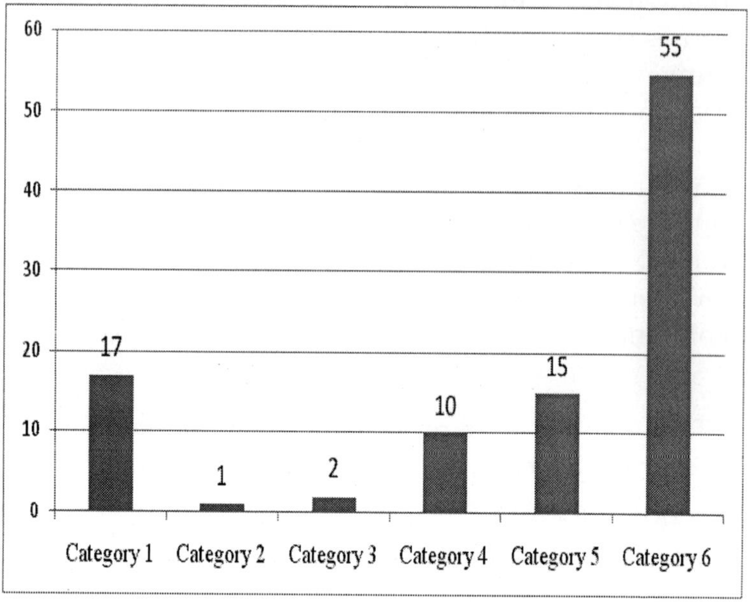

Note: Category 1= Ethnic identity crisis of the Rajbanshis, Category 2= Wrong policies of the government, Category 3= Impact of modern civilization, Category 4= undeveloped, Category 5= Cooch Behar merger in West Bengal in 1950 and Category 6= All the Above.

If we see the responses of the respondents it is obvious that though all the factors mentioned in the above are responsible for Greater Cooch Behar movement but three emerge as the most important factors responsible for Greater Cooch Behar movement are ethnic identity crisis of the Koch Rajbanhis, wrong policies of the government and Cooch Behar Merger in West Bengal on 1950. As an ethnic community, Koch Rajbanshis have their own distinct culture, language, and identity but due to several causes like domination of the dominant groups, impact of modern civilization, indifference of the government policies, etc, they are losing their distinctiveness. Undeveloped is another problem. It started the early part of the 90s for the land alienation and continued to the present day. The land alienation emerged as a major problem among the Rajbanshis in North Bengal mainly due to migration of the upper caste Hindu Bengalis from the other parts of West Bengal as well as immigration from the Bangladesh to the Rajbanshis inhabited areas that was a major cause which created a sense of alienation among them and compelled them to think for preservation of their distinctiveness. In the case of Assam, this problem emerged after the 1980s as a major challenge due to illegal infiltration from Bangladesh to the lower parts of Assam where most of the areas are Rajbanshi dominated. Therefore, it is evident that in the anti-immigration movement of West Bengal the contribution of the Rajbanshis is much more prominent.

Though a small number of respondents (3 percent) felt about the impact of modern civilization on the Kamatapur movement that is an important point that they have raised. Globalization, cultural hybridization, cultural fusion, etc are some remarkable world phenomenon that the world has experience today. Globalization is trying to make the world into a global village where everything will be the same for all. Cultural hybridization is optimistic to make a common culture that is acceptable for all and which will decrease the cultural distinction and conflict over culture and identity. But it is contradictory to be optimistic to consider the cultural hybridity as a solution to the problem of conflict over culture and identity, as the world is witnessing many ethnic-based identity conflicts over the years. Koch Rajbanshi's identity movement is also one of them. To achieve and fulfill the basic economic requirement of life, Globalization, cultural hybridization, and cultural fusion are pushing the smaller ethnic groups to accept it but at the same time, it has created a consciousness and fear of losing their traditional cultural values, language and identity. Therefore, they have started to rethink and re-establish their traditional cultural values and identity.

Another response of the Cooch Behar Merger in the West Bengal in 1950 was a very important cause origin of the movement.

As regards the question of what kind of major challenges the Rajbanshis are confronted at present, the response of the respondents was varying as shown in the table below (Table-11). Eleven (11) percent of respondents opined that ethnic identity crisis is a major challenge that the Rajbanshis are confronted with. Two (2) percent opined that illiteracy is a major problem that the Rajbanshis are facing at present. Similarly, nine (9) percent of the respondents identified economic underdevelopment as a major challenge of the Rajbanshis. Considering all the facts seventy-eight (78) percent of respondents considered all the above-mentioned factors as a major challenge presently confronting the Rajbanshis.

Table-11: Tabular representation of the Respondent's Opinion about the major challenges the Rajbanshis are confronted at present

Major challenges the Rajbanshis are confronted at present	*No. of respondents*	*Percentage*
Ethnic identity crisis	11	11
Illiteracy	2	2
Economic under-development	9	9
All the above	78	78
Total	100	100

As far as the responses of the respondents are concerned the Rajbanshi community of West Bengal is facing many problems. From the point of view of the Greater Cooch Behar movement, they are facing problems related to the problem of socio-cultural development and political identity, illiteracy, poverty, etc.

Figure-21: Bar Diagram showing the Respondents' Opinion about the Major Challenges the Rajbanshis are confronted at Present (in Percent)

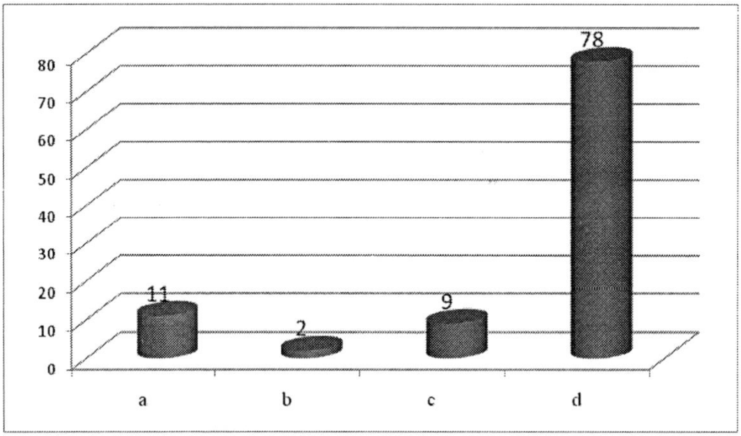

Note: a= Ethnic identity crisis, b= Illiteracy, c= Underdevelopment, d= All the above.

In order to assess the perception of the respondents with regard to the possible solution of the Rajbanshis problem, the response to the question was varying as shown in the table below (Table-12). The respondents were asked to identify the possible solution of the Rajbanshis problem from the options. Five (5) percent of the total respondents felt that the preservation and development of Rajbanshis cultural, language, etc is one step that can be taken as a possible solution to the Rajbanshis problem while twelve (12) percent of the respondents opined that economic development of the Rajbanahis is an urgent need to solve the problem of Rajbanshis. On the other hand, twenty (20) percent of the respondents opined that the creation of separate the Greater Cooch Behar or Kamatapur state is the only solution to the Rajbanshis problem. Similarly, three (3) percent suggested that more amenities/improvements for the government facility of the Rajbanshis peoples will be an important step for bringing the solution to the Rajbanshis problem. However, sixty (60) percent of the respondents opined that the all the above-mentioned steps (reservation and development of Rajbanshis cultural, language, etc, economic development of the Rajbanshis, creation of separate the Greater Cooch Behar or kamatapur state, and more improvements of Rajbanshi peoples) should be taken for bringing solution to the Rajbanshis problem.

Table-12: Tabular representation of Respondents' Opinion regarding the possible solution to the Rajbanshis problem

A possible solution to the Rajbanshis problem	*No. of respondents*	*Percentage*
Reservation and development of Rajbanshi cultural, language, etc	7	7
The economic development of Rajbanshis	13	13
Creation of separate Greater Cooch Behar/Kamatapur state	20	20
More improvements for a government facility	3	3
All the above	60	60
Total	100	100

Figure-22: Bar Diagram showing the Respondents' Opinion regarding the Possible Solution of the Rajbanshis Problem (in percent)

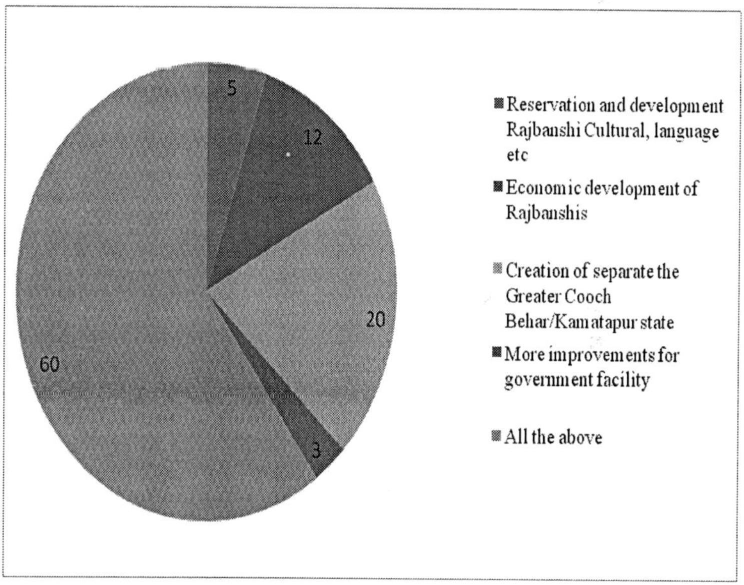

Finally, from the above responses of the respondents, it may be said that the problem of the Rajbanshis does not lie in any single factor. They have been facing many problems since independence. Different issues are required to be resolved to bring a permanent solution to their problems. Economic development of Rajbanshis, reservation and development of Rajbanshis socio-cultural, linguistic and political identity, more improvements for government facility and if Greater Cooch Behar is not possible then creation of autonomous council where they at least get some amount of autonomy of self-rule are some remarkable steps should be taken for bringing solution to the problems of Rajbanshis.

REFERENCES

Ananda Bazar Prtrika: on 25 Aug 2016.

Barman, Rup Kumar (2003), *Contested Regionalism: A New Look on the History, Cultural Change and Regionalism of North Bengal and Lower Assam,* Abhijeet Publications, Delhi.

Das, Naren (2007), UTJAS: A Dalit Student Movement, in Sukhbilash Barma (ed.), *Socio-Political Movements in North Bengal: A Sub-Himalayan Tract,* Global Vision Publishing House, New Delhi.

Debnath, Sailen (2016), *The Koch-Rajbanshis from Panchanan to Greater Cooch Behar Movement,* Aayu Publication, New Delhi.

Jana, Arun Kumar (2010), Backwardness and Political Articulation of Backwardness in the north Bengal region of West Bengal, in Asutosh Kumar (ed.), *Rethinking State Politics in India, Region within Region,* Routledge.

Ray, Haripada (2007), The Genesis of Uttar Khanda Movements, in Sukhbilas Barma (ed.), *Socio-Political movements in North Bengal: A Sub-Himalayan Tract,* Global Vision Publishing House, New Delhi.

Uttar Banga Sambad on 20 Sept 2005, 23 Feb. 2016.

Conclusion

The present study *"Rajbanshi Peoples and Greater Cooch Behar Movement in West Bengal"* is an attempt to study the statehood movement of the Rajbanshis in West Bengal. Apart from its significant impact on the socio-political history of West Bengal, the Greater Cooch Behar movement is instrumental to a very large extent in bringing similar identity aspirations among other communities in West Bengal. To understand the problem a field study was conducted during the month of January and February 2017. With this purpose, the adequate size of the sample was drawn from different socio-cultural and literary organizations including the common people who could throw light on this issue. Moreover, this work has been done keeping in mind all probable aspects related to the problem while analyzing the relevant Government official documents, News Papers and interpretations of different people of the Rajbanshi community many of whom directly involved with the movement.

The Rajbanshis are one of the oldest aboriginal ethnic groups of South Asia having predominantly mixed features (*Aryan-Mongoloid-Dravidian*). Historical sources adequately bring out the fact of social mobility among the autochthones in different forms including the emergence of new castes in the social claim of North-Eastern Bengal and parts of Assam. The Rajbanshis appellation and the claim of *kshatriya* status go back to the early historical period. The colonial administration-ethnographers like Gait, Hutton, Dalton, Risley, and Thompson were unanimously supported that a section of Koch of Northern Bengal began to call themselves 'Rajbanshi' from the early 19th century. But there was also a belief among others that all the Rajbanshis were not Koch. Some of them were Dravidian and not Mongoloid like the Koches.

Historical sources adequately bring out the fact of social mobility among the autochthones in different forms including the emergence of new castes in the social claim of North-Eastern Bengal and parts of Assam. The Rajbanshis appellation and the claim of *kshatriya* status go back to the early historical period.19 The colonial administration-ethnographers like Gait, Hutton, Dalton, Risley, and Thompson were unanimously supported that a section of Koch of Northern Bengal began to call themselves *'Rajbanshi'* from the early 191 h century. But there was also a belief among others that all the Rajbanshis were not Koch. Some of them were Dravidian and not Mongoloid like the Koches the appellation of the great bulk of the admittedly Hindu population in their neighborhood. Hodgson takes down the physiognomy of the Koches as verily similar to the physical traits of the Mongoloid and thus regard them as Mongoloid. He also says, "Biswa Singh, Hajo's grandson became Hindu, renounced the name Koch and adopted Rajbanshi". Bravery calls it a Rajbanshi and Palia is the same ethnic group of people. This ethnic group is not *Aryan* but its origins from the king of *Dravidian-Bhutanese* family, says Dalton. However, 0' Donnel says, "Another interesting tribe is the Rajbanshi or Koch of North-Eastern Bengal, the localization of whose racial position has long been a subject of dispute. They are, however, only the third wave of *Mongoloid* who have advanced through the eastern passes in the first being the Chandal, the second the Koch and the last the *Ahom*." It assumes that this ethnic group of people's blood is a mixture of Dravidian-Austro-Mongolian impacts to be black or coppery. This group of people has small eyes, straight hair- a broad jaw. There are yellow and white color people among the Rajbanshis. Dr. Cham Chandra Sanyal has dealt with this issue in his work *The Rajbansis of North Bengal* in detail. Thus most of the colonial administrators and ethnographers and some of the Indian scholars tried to establish that the Koches and the Rajbanshis are the same racial group.

On the other hand, the Indian scholars like Maniram Kavyabhusan, Harikishore Adhikary, Manbhola Ray, Upendra Nath Barman, S.K.Chatterjee and others tried to refer that the Rajbanshis were different from the Koches and the formers were superior to the later. The Rajbanshis were the indigenous Hindu inhabitant than before the reign of Viswa Singh adopted Hinduism. This view is also supported in the religious and cannon literature like Puranas, *Tantrcis, the Ramayan, the Mahabharata, etc.* In Chapter No. I (one) has been discussed in detail. On the basis of selected anthropometric observations, Atul Sur comes to the conclusion that in the Jalpaiguri, there was the considerable admixture of the Rajbanshi with the Mongoloid blood; whereas, in West Dinajpur, the *Desi* Rajbanshi had intermingled with the Dravidian race. However, the ethnic affinity of the Rajbanshi with the Koch is still a matter of mystery. In addition, on the identity question, several controversial statements have been noted that ultimately instead of simplifying the problem, have made the issue more cop1plicated and sensitive. This issue became more complicated when the Rajbanshi claimed ethnic-cum-caste identity and differentiate themselves from the Koches.

Hiuen Tsang and S. K. Chatterjee have observed that the whole of Bengal including the Northern part adopted the Aryan language and culture by the 7th century. While assuming the views for some difference between the language of Kamrup and that of Middle India, as alluded by Hiuen Tsang, he has says that *Kamatapuri language* has *Tibeto-Burman* elements and as such the Aryan language has been a bit distorted by Kamrup pronunciation.

The endeavor of the Rajbanshi to be placed higher up in order of precedence and be recognized as *kshatriya* continued from 1872 A.D. to 1931A.D. census assuming new names viz., from *Koch* to *Rajbanshi* (1872), from *Rajbanshi* to *Bratya I Bhanga Kshatriya* (1891), from *Braiya Kshatriya* to *Rajbanshi Kshatriya* (1911 and 1921) and from *Rajbanshi Kshatriya* to only *Kshatriya* (1931). The Rajbanshi presumed that if they could succeed in getting themselves recorded as *Kshatriya* in the census, an official document of the Government no one would indeed be able to dispute their rank in the caste hierarchy. Further to confirmed their Kshatriya identity, there were serious efforts on the part of the

Rajbanshi leaders to secure the opinion of Brahmin *Pandits* of Nabadwip and Ben eras and other *shastric* sanctions from them to validate that claim.

They also wanted to get it legitimized by the priests and genealogists. Mythology and traditions were also frequently cited in support of their claim to be recognized as descendants of *Kshatriya Varna.* Attempts were being made to recognize *kshatriyahood* as by the Rajbanshi taking the materials from folk tales, folk songs, legends, proverbs, etc. For some kind of institutional support to their endeavor to get recognized as Kshatriya and also for mass mobilization, they also founded *Kshatriya Samiti* in 1910 at Rangpur. It was Panchanan Barma under whose leadership the *Kshatriya Samiti* not only put forward claim to higher social status but also urged their members to abandon many of the practices considered degrading by the upper castes have been discussed in the Chapter No. II (two).

The historical memory of Kamatapur state and Cooch Behar kingdom is important to know the historical process of Rajbanshs identity formation. In the contemporary social and political discourse, the Rajbanshis feel proud to identify themselves with Kamatapur and are fighting for the reconstruction of their Kamatapur state which is rooted in history. History says that the Rajbanshi kingdom in Kamatapur was there for a long period of time from the 13th century onwards and disappeared in the process of post-independent state formation in India with the Indian state of Assam, West Bengal and partly in Bangladesh. It is believed that in the 13th century Sandhya Rai established the kingdom of Kamata also known as Kamrup Kamata comprising many parts of present Northeast India and continued till the 15th century.

It was in the 16th century when Rajbanshis emerged as a strong and influential kingdom established by Bishwa Singha who ruled over Kamata from 1515 to 1540. The region of Bishwa Singha's Dynasty rule was known as the Cooch Behar Kingdom but in the course of time, this kingdom went through various names and lastly named Cooch Behar (Koch Bihar) in the colonial period. The Dynasty established by Bishwa Singha continued till the middle part of the 18th century with various ups and downs and many Koch kings ruled over the Kamatapur kingdom. Dharmendra Narayan was the last king of Bishwa Singha's Dynasty. During this period the attacks of the Bhutanese were increased in the politics of the Kamata kingdom. Bhutanese king directly interfered with Koch affairs and the kingdom at Koch Behar. To get rid of the Bhutanese attacks king Dharmendra Narayan signed one treaty with East India Company on 5th April 1773. As a result of this treaty the Koch-Kamata alias, Cooch Behar kingdom became a native state under colonial India and continued till 1947. According to the Indian Independence Act, section VIII, Cooch Behar -Kamata kingdom alias Cooch Behar gained its independence from British rule and the treaty of 1773 became invalid. Till 28 August 1949 Koch Behar was an Indian State ruled by Maharaja Jagadipendra Narayan. On 28 August 1949 by an agreement Maharaja Jagaddipendra Narayan king of Cooch Behar ceded his state with the Dominion of the Government of India. The administrative power on Koch Behar was transferred to the Government of India on 12th September 1949 and from that time onwards Cooch Behar was ruled as a Chief Commissioner's Province. But on 1st January 1950, Cooch Bihar was transferred and merged with the Indian state of West Bengal.

The merger of Cooch Behar as a district in the state of West Bengal was a starting point that gave rise to separate Statehood among the Rajbanshis. Many Rajbanshi civil and political organizations argue that the merger of Cooch Behar was against the will of the people and was a conspiracy of the government of West Bengal and the government of India. Socio-political organizations that were born out immediately after the merger of Cooch Behar, *Hitasadhini Sabha* argued that Cooch Behar should not be merged with either Bengal or Assam, rather it should be a union territory under thc control of the central government. UKDs leaders say that the merger of Cooch Behar was the beginning and main factor which has disturbed the unity of the greater Rajbanshi community. Even till today, this is the main argument rises by most of the Rajbanshis socio-political organizations like *Greater Cooch Behar Peoples' Association* that are demanding and agitating for a separate Greater Cooch Behar state and this movement supported Indian national political party BJP.

Rajbanshis' separate state movement is a long drawn battle to preserve protect and develop their distinct identity. The genesis of the Kamatapur movement or Rajbanshis nationalism was in the colonial period. The issue of development of Rajbanshi language and its consciousness also arose during the colonial period. After the independence of India, identity assertion emerged amongst the Rajbanshis due to the merger of the kingdom of Cooch Behar with the Indian state of West Bengal against the will of the local peoples. After the merger, many socio-political organizations were formed both in Assam as well as in North Bengal and still agitating for a separate Greater Cooch Behar state and socio-cultural as well as economic development of their community. Their proposed state of Greater Cooch Behar consisted of 4 districts of Assam and 6 districts of North Bengal.

Apart from the creation of a separate state of Greater Cooch Behar the autonomy movement by the Rajbanshis also looks for the recognition of *Kamatapuri or Rajbanshi language* under the Eight Scheduled of the Constitution of India. In the case of Assam, the movement also demands Scheduled Tribe status for the Rajbanshis living in North Bengal and Assam. Scheduling the Rajbanshi community in the category of ST is a long-standing demand. Since long, particularly from 1966, many Rajbanshi socio-cultural organizations have been demonstrating and agitating in support of their demand. But yet this demand has not been addressed by the Government. Now in North Bengal, the Scheduling issue of the Rajbanshi is entirely politicized by the national as well as by the regional parties. It is observed that though the root of the historical origin of the Kamatapur movement was in the colonial period in the case of West Bengal the movement got its momentum after the 1980s only. It was because of the expression of the frustration of the peoples on the politics played by the government towards their demand for Schedule Tribe status.

One point needs to be underscored that though the historical reasons for claiming Greater Cooch Behar is similar in Assam as well as in North Bengal, yet there are some factors which contributed a lot to the Greater Cooch Behar movement in West Bengal. Issues of poverty, economic disparities, identity crisis, and relative deprivation are some important factor that has given a new shape to the *Greater Cooch Behar movement* in North Bengal.

At present Rajbanshis are confronted by problems ranging from an ethnic identity crisis, economic underdevelopment, land alienation, illiteracy, unemployment, etc. Most of the Rajbanshis in North Bengal are living below the poverty line. No policy measure has been taken by the government to uplift their economic conditions. The claim for ST status is a long drawn demand. They were in hope that if they get the ST status they will at least be able to get some opportunities for their socio-economic and cultural development. But they are deprived of that too.

It may be safely argued that the Greater Cooch Behar movement is in many ways the outcome of the socio-political and economic marginalization of Rajbanshis. Rajbanshis who once ruled over large parts of Northeast India suffered economic hardship and political marginalization due to the attack from Bhutias and to get rid of this they came under British India as a native state. After the merger of their princely state Cooch Behar with the Indian state of West Bengal they systematically became victims of socio-cultural and economic marginalization that has created a feeling of alienation, deprivation, and fear of losing their distinct identity. In the early part of the 20th century, their culture and language suffered due to the caste movement that aimed at assimilation of Rajbanshis with the upper castes. During that time in North Bengal, the immigration of upper-caste Hindu Bengalis to the Rajbanshi dominated areas created tension among the native Rajbanshis. They were victims of social-cultural discrimination and domination by the upper caste Assamese in Assam and Bengalis in North Bengal. Their social identity suffered due to colonial caste policies which led them to fight for caste solidarity. Today the Greater Cooch Behar movement is trying to create a separate state (own rule) on the basis of their identity, culture, and language. This will help them to justify their claim of geographically demarcated land so that they can arrange the resources of this region for their own development. Similarly, they are also trying to mobilize people's consciousness towards their history, culture, and tradition to ensure their socio-cultural development.

As regards the future of the *Greater Cooch Behar movement* it may be said that the movement will continue till the basic problems of the Rajbanshis are addressed. The community members who are leading the Greater Cooch Behar movement instead of mobilizing on the basis of their identity, culture, and language needs to search solution in development and good governance. Considering all the findings during the course of the present study it may be suggested that several steps may be taken to address the problems of Rajbanshis. Firstly, it is of urgent importance to conduct a survey of the social, economic and political conditions of the Rajbanshis of North-east India. Such a survey will help us to understand the socio-economic and political problems that Rajbanshis have been facing. Any kind of policy aimed to address the issues related to this community is bound to fail if we do not have a clear understanding of their socio-economic and political conditions. Secondly, immediate steps should be taken to preserve and protect the peculiarities and particularities of this community. The feeling of alienation and relative deprivation can be addressed only by protecting their very distinctiveness and by improving socio-cultural and economic conditions. Thirdly, the language controversy is another important issue. To put an end to the debate on Rajbanshi/ Kamatapuri language and their aspiration to develop, their mother tongue should be given constitutional recognition. Fifthly, the economic development of the region should be accelerated. As most Rajbanshis live in abject conditions of poverty, certain political-economic measures have to be taken urgently for the economic security of the Rajbanshis living below the poverty line. Along with this, spreading quality education and the creation of employment avenues may go a long way in solving such problems. Moreover, Rajbanshis should get their socioeconomic and political dues to be governed by them as a true democracy in India.

The present study has some limitations. The study did not make a comparative analysis of Rajbanshis separate state movement with other such movements in Northeast India. Another limitation is that the present study mainly focuses on the socio-cultural identity of Rajbanshis. It could not look into the political as well as the economic problem of the community. Another concern is the role of women. Women have made a considerable contribution in the course of the Greater Cooch Behar movement but it was also not covered in the present study. To conclude it may be said that the Indian state has not been able to address the multi-cultural, multi-ethnic and multi-lingual problems of the local peoples living in India. In the case of North-east India, particularly in North Bengal, the Central, as well as the State government, has failed to resolve the ethnic problems, the ongoing ethnic conflicts by the various ethnic communities in West Bengal including the Rajbanshis. The statehood movement by these ethnic groups has thrown up issues of terrorism, economic stagnancy, cultural threats, human rights violation, political instability to name a few. To maintain national integrity, political stability and socio-economic development of the state, it is an urgent need and responsibility of the Indian state to address the multilayered problems that the ethnic and tribal groups of West Bengal have been facing.

Bibliography

Acharya, N. N. (1996), *A Brief History of Assam: From earliest time to the year 1983*, Omsons Publications, Guwahati.

Adhikary, Madhab Chandra (2014), *Rajbanshi Samaj O Manishi Panchanan Barma (Bengali)*, Reader Service, Kolkata.

Adhikary, Harikishore (1314 BS), *Rajbanshi Kula Pradeep (Bengali)*, Calcutta.

Ahamed, Kha Chowdhari Amanatulla (1990), *Cooch Beharer Itihas (Bengali)*, Modern Book Agency Pvt. Ltd., Kolkata.

Ananda Bazar Patrika: on 25 Aug 2016.

Barman, Rup Kumar (2007), *Contested Regionalism: A New Look on the History, Cultural Change and Regionalism of North Bengal and Lower Assam*, Abhijeet Publications, Delhi.

Barma, Sukhbilash (2004), *Indian Folk Music Bhawaiya Ethnomusicological study*, Global Vision Publishing House, New Delhi.

Barman, Kartick Chandra (2015), *Social Reforms Activities of Manishi Panchanan Barma towards Rajbanshi Society: A Brief Historical Perspective*, North Asian International Research Journal of Social Science and Humanities, NAISRJC, Vol.-1, Issue-2.

Barman, Kartick Chandra (2015), *Social Philosophy of Manishi Panchanan Barma: A Brief Study on Historical Perspectives*, IJARIIE, Vol-1, Issue- 4.

Barman, Kartick Chandra (2015), *Economics Thought of Panchanan Barma and Kshatriya Bank: A Brief on Historical Perspective*, Historical Research, Science Publishing Group.

Barman, Upendra Nath (1941), *Rajbanshi Kshatriya Jatir Itihas (Bengali)*, Jalpaiguri.

Barman, Upendra Nath (1401 BS), *Kshatriya Jatir Itihas*, Jalpaiguri.

Barman, Upendra Nath (1379 BS), *Thakur Panchanan Barmar Jibon Charit*, Jalpaiguri.

Basu, Durga Das (1980), *Introduction to The Constitution of India* (eight editions), Prentice Hall of India Pvt. Ltd., New Delhi.

Basu, Swaraj (2003), *Dynamics of a Caste Movement: The Rajbansis of North Bengal 1910-1947*, Manohar Publication, New Delhi.

Berevly, H. (1872), *Census Report of Bengal*, Vol.- I.

Bhamaritantra, 2nd stanza.

Chowdhury, H. N. (1903), *Cooch Behar State and its Land Revenue Settlement*, State Book Press, Cooch Behar.

Choudhuri, Arjun (2013), *Koch and Rajbanshi: Confusion or Fusion*, Net link:- https://www.koch

rajbanshicentre.org/2013/09/16/Koch_and_rajbansi_confusion_or_fusion. Access on 15 January 2017.

Census of India (1921). Net link: http://www.censusindia.gov.in/census_and_you/old_report/censu-1921.aspx. Access on 20 January 2017.

Dalton, E. T. (1872), *Descriptive Ethnology of Bengal*, Office of the Superintendent of Government Printing, Calcutta.

Das, Arup Jyoti (2009), *Kamatapur and the Koch Rajbanshi Imagination*, Arunima Deka Publication, Guwahati.

Das, Dhirendra Nath (2005), *Regional Movements, Ethnicity and Politics*, Abhijeet Publications, Delhi.

Das, Sukumar (1982), *Uttarbanger Itihas (Bengali)*, Kumar Sahitya Prokashan, Kolkata.

Das, Naren (2007), *UTJAS: A Dalit Student Movement*, in Sukhbilash Barma (ed.), Socio-Political Movements in North Bengal: A Sub-Himalayan Tract, Global Vision Publishing House, New Delhi.

Das, Pran Gobinda (2013), *Bharatio Rastro Chinta O Jatio Andolon*, NCBA, Kolkata.

Datta, D. (2013), *King Nara Narayana's Military Campaigning in North-East India: An Analysis Through Numismatics*, The NEHU Journal, Vol. XI, No. 1. PP-35-43.

Deb, Ranajit (2014), *Cooch Behar Zelar Itihas (Bengali)*, Purbottar Prokashan, Cooch Behar.

Deb, Saswati (2016), *Cooch Beharer Raj Kahini-O-Rajprasad*, Tribitta Prokashan, Cooch Behar.

Debnath, Sailen (2010), *The Doars in Historical Transition*, N. L. Publication, Siliguri.

Debnath, Sailen (2016), *The Koch-Rajbanshis from Panchanan to Greater Cooch Behar Movement*, Aayu, Publication, New Delhi.

Dey, Andhendu Mouli (1420 BS), *Rai Saheb Panchana Barmar Kshatriya Andolon (Bengali)*, in Goswami, Kamalesh (ed.), Bidrpoha-O-Andolane Uttarbanga, Priya Book House, Kolkata.

Gupta, Ashok Das (2013), *Queruing Relevance of the Term 'Indigenous Peoples' in a Three-Level-Approach with Special Reference to Rajbanshi Community of North Bengal*, West Bengal, India, International E-Publication, Palhar Nagar.

Gupta, Dipankar (2000), *Interrogating Caste: Understanding Hierarchy and difference in Indian Society*, Penguin Publication, New Delhi.

Gait, E. A. (2011), *A History of Assam*, Guwahati, Spectrum Publication, Delhi.

Ghosal, Sarat Chandra (1942), *A History of Cooch Behar*, Cooch Behar State Press, Cooch Behar. Hadgson, B. H. (1949), On the Origin Location, Numbers, Creed, Customs, Character and Condition of Koch, Bodo and Dhimal People; with General description of the climate they dwell, in Journal of Asiatic Society of Bengal, Vol. XVIII, Part.- II.

Hamilton, Buchanon (1810), *Account of the District of Rangpur*, Appendix- III of the District Census Handbook, Jalpaiguri and Cooch Behar, West Bengal, 1915.

Hunter, Dr. (1872), *Statistical Account of Cooch Behar*, N. L. Publication, Siliguri.

Hunter, Dr. W. W. (1876), *A Statistical Account of Bengal*, Vol. X, Concept Publishing Company, New Delhi.

Jana, Arun Kumar (2010), *Backwardness and Political Articulation of Backwardness in the north Bengal region of West Bengal*, in Asutosh Kumar (ed.), Rethinking state politics in India, region within region, Routlodge.

Mukhopadyaya, Subodh Kumar (2001), *Economic History of Bengal*, Kolkata.

Majumder, R. C. (2011), *History of Bengal*, Vol. I. BR Publishing Corporation, Delhi.

Nandi, Rajib (2014), *Spectacles of Ethnographic and Historical Imaginations: Kamatapur Movement and the Rajbanshi Quest to Rediscover Their Past and Selves*, History and Anthropology, Vol. 25, No. 5, pp. 571-591.

Nath, D. (1989), *History of Koch Kingdom*, Mittal Publication, New Delhi.

O'Malley, L.S.S. (1911), *Census Report of India*, Vol- V, Part-I(Bengal).

Porter, A. E. (1931), *Census of India*, Vol.- V, Part- I. Rajkhowa, J. P. (2001), Generalissimo Chilarai and His Times, Vikram Publishers, Guwahati.

Panchayat Raj Patrika 2016.

Ray, Haripada (2007), *The Genesis of Uttar Khanda Movements*, in Sukhbilas Barma (ed.), *Socio-Political movements in North Bengal: A Sub-Himalayan Tract*, Global Vision Publishing House, New Delhi.

Roy, Manomohan (1902), *Some Notes on the Rajbanshi*, Journal of Asiatic Society of Bengal, Kolkata, Vol.- LXXI, No.- 2.

Roy, Nalini Ranjan (2007), *Koch Kingdom and Kamatapur: the Truth Unveiled*, Vicky Publication, Guwahati.

Risely, H. H. (1891), *The Tribes and Castes of Bengal*, Vol.-I, Bengal Secretariat Press, Calcutta.

Samaddar, Ranabir (1985), *Bharater Jatio Andolon O Jatio Sanghatir Samasyad (Bengali)*, West Bengal State Book, Kolkata.

Sengupta, Dr. Gitashree Bandhana (1999), *Spondita Antarlik*, progreesive publication, Kolkata.

Singha, Kshetra Nath (2004), *Rai Saheb Panchanan Barmar Jibani* (Bengali), Dr. Nripendra Nath Pal (ed.), Anima Prakashani, Kolkata.

Sanyal, Charu Chandra (1965), *The Rajbansis of North Bengal*, The Asiatic Society, Kolkata.

Singha, Khetra Nath (2011), *Rai Saheb Panchanan Barmar Jiboni (Bengali)*, Dr. Nripendranatth Pal (ed.), Anima Prakashani, Kolkata.

Tarkaratna, Panchanan (1384 BS), *Kalika Purana*, Nababharat Publishers, Kolkata.

Thomson, W. H. (1921), *Census Report of India*, Vol.-V, Part- I (Bengal).

Uttar Banga Sambad on 20 Sept 2005, 23 Feb 2016.

Waddle, L. A. (1975), *Tribes of the Brahmaputra Valley*, Read Books, Delhi.

Appendix-A

(Interview Schedule)

Sl. No. .... Date ....

1. Name –
2. Guardian Name-
3. Age-
4. Occupation-
5. Education Qualification-
6. Gender-
7. Address.....
8. Caste- (a) Rajbanshi (b) Others
9. Religion- (a) Hindu (b) Others
10. Mothers Tague—(a) Kamatapuri/Kamrupi (b) Bengali (c) Others
11. Do you support the Greater Cooch Behar Movement/ Kamatapur Movement:

    (a) Yes (b) No
12. You are involved in this movement: (a) Direct (b) Indirect (c) No involve
13. Who are the supporters of the Greater Cooch Behar Movement?

    (a) Only Rajbanshis Peoples

    (b) Others Peoples
14. What is the state government's response towards the movement?

    (a) Positive

    (b) Negative

    (c) Partially positive.
15. What is the central Government's Response towards the movement?

    (a) Positive

(b) Negative

(c) Partially positive

16. What are the causes responsible for the Greater Cooch Behar movement?

    (a) The ethnic identity crisis of the Rajbanshis.

    (b) Wrong policies of Government

    (c) Impact of modern civilization

    (d) Underdevelopment

    (e) Cooch Behar merger in West Bengal on 1950

    (d) All the above.

17. What kind of major challenges the Rajbanshis are confronted at present?

    (a) Ethnic identity crisis

    (b) Illiteracy

    (c) Economic underdevelopment

    (d) All the above.

18. What is the possible solution stop of the Greater Cooch Behar Movement?

    (a) Preservation and development of the Rajbansi culture, language, etc.

    (b) The economic development of Rajbanshi

    (c) Creation of separate Greater Cooch Behar state.

    (d) More facility of Government policy.

    (c) All the above.

19. Do you have any comment on the present condition of Rajbanshis?

20. Do you have any comment on the Greater Cooch Behar movement?

Appendix B

Cooch Behar Merger Agreement

The agreement made this twenty-eighth day of August 1949 between the Governor-General of India and His Highness the Maharaja of Cooch Behar.

Whereas in the best interests of the State of Cooch Behar as well as of the Dominion of India it is desirable to provide for the administration of the said State by or under the authority of the Dominion Government:

It is hereby agreed as follows: ~

Article -1:-

His Highness the Maharaja of Cooch Behar hereby cedes to the Dominion Government full and exclusive authority, jurisdiction and powers for and in relation to the governance of the State and agrees to transfer the administration of the State to the Dominion Government on the 12th day of September 1949 (hereinafter referred to as the said day).

As from the said day the Dominion Government will be competent to exercise the said powers, authority and jurisdiction in such manner and through such agency as it may think fit.

Article - 2:-

His Highness the Maharaja shall continue to enjoy the same personal rights, privileges, dignities, and titles which he would have enjoyed had this agreement not been made.

Article - 3:-

His Highness the Maharaja shall with effect from the said day is entitled to receive for his lifetime from the revenues of the State annually for his privy purse the sum of Rupees eight lakhs fifty thousand free of all taxes. After him, the privy parts will be fixed at Rupees seven lakhs only. this amount is intended to cover all the expenses of the Ruler and his family, including expenses on account of his personal staff, maintenance of his residences, marriages and other ceremonies, etc., and will neither be increased nor reduced for any reason whatsoever.

The Government of India undertakes the said sum of Rupees eight lakhs fifty thousand shall be paid to His Highness the Maharaja in four equal installments in advance at the beginning of each quarter from the State Treasury or at such Treasury as may be specified by the Government of India.

Article - 4:-

His Highness the Maharaja shall be entitled to the full ownership, use, and enjoyment of all private properties (as distinct from State properties) belonging to him on the date of this agreement. His Highness the Maharaja will furnish to the Dominion Government before the 15th September 1949, an inventory of all the immovable property, securities and cash balances held by him as such private property. If any dispute arises as to whether any item of property is the private property of His Highness the Maharaja or State property, it shall be referred to a Judicial Officer qualified to be appointed as High Court Judge, and the decision of that officer shall be final and binding on both parties.

Article - 5:-

All the members of His Highness' family shall be entitled to all the personal privileges, dignities and titles enjoyed by them whether within or outside the territories of the State, immediately before the 15th day of August 1947.

Article - 6:-

The Dominion Government guarantees the succession, according to law and custom, to the Gaddi of the State and to His Highness the Maharaja's personal rights, privileges, dignities and titles.

Article - 7:-

No inquiry shall be made by or under the authority of the Government of India, and no proceedings shall lie in any court in Cooch Behar against His Highness the Maharaja, whether in a personal capacity or otherwise, in respect of anything done or omitted to be done by him or under his authority during the period of his administration of that State.

Article - 8:-

(i) The Government of India hereby guarantees either the continuants in service of the permanent members of the public services of Cooch Behar on conditions which will be not less advantageous than those on which they were serving before the date on which the administration of Cooch Behar is made over to the Government of India or the payment of reasonable compensation.

(ii) The Government of India further guarantees the continuance of pensions and leave salaries sanctioned by His Highness the Maharaja to servants of the State who have etired or proceed on leave preparatory to retirement, before the date on which the administration of Cooch Behar is made over to the Government of India.

Article - 9:-

Except with the previous sanction of the Government of India no proceedings, civil and criminal, shall be instituted against any person in respect of any act done or purpoting to be done in the execution of his duties as a servant of the State before the day on which the administration is made over to the Government of India. In confirmation whereof Mr. Vapal Pangunni Menon, Advisor to the Govt. of India in the Ministry of States has appended his signature on behalf and with the authority of the Governor-General of India and Lieutenant Colonel His Highness the Maharaja Jagaddipendra Narayan Bhup Bahadur, Maharaja of Cooch Behar, has appended his signature on behalf of himself, his heirs and successors.

Jagaddipendra Narayan
Maharaja of Cooch Behar

V. P. Menon
Advisor to the Govt. of India
Ministry of States

Appendix C

The demand for Kamatapur Peoples' Party

The KPP or Kamtapur Peoples' Party on 26.09.97 submitted a memorandum to the Prime Minister of India, Indrakumar Gujral, through the divisional commissioner of North Bengal, Jalpaiguri division. The 11 points charter of demands were —

1. In order to enable the Kamtapuri speaking people to govern their own lives by reason of ethnic, linguistic, historical, cultural and social distinction from the rest of the people of West Bengal a separate statehood namely 'KAMTAPUR' be created within the framework of India comprising the whole of North Bengal and adjoining Kamtapuri populated areas in India, in accordance with the article (3) of the Constitution of India.
2. With a view to advancing the language of the Kamtapuris, it is included in the 8th schedule of the Constitution of India.
3. On the basis of the lease-year of 1971 (Indira-Mujib accord), the expulsion of illegal foreigners from the Kamptapuri areas of North Bengal is implemented soon.
4. In order to curb the illegal influx of immigrants in North Bengal and adjacent Kamtapuri dominated areas, the 'INNER & PERMIT LINE' must immediately be imposed on the said areas.

5. With a view to restraining the intrusion of illegal foreigners in North Bengal, barbed wire is erected on the borderline of both India and Bangladesh without further delay.
6. Regarding various cultural programmes of Kamtapurians for the Kamtapuri people of North Bengal should be arranged to telecast on the television by opening Fulbari Doordarshan substation centre immediately.
7. With a view to ensuring an all round development of North Bengal, the Teesta irrigation project should be immediately declared as a national project.
8. In order to enrich the culture of the Kamtapuri people of North Bengal as well as neighbouring areas, different types of cultural programmes of Kamtapurians be broadcast through All India Radio, Siliguri at par with daily the programmes in Nepali by the All India Radio, Kurseong.
9. In respect of promoting higher education for the aboriginal people of North Bengal a central university namely Roy Saheb Thakur Panchanan Barma University is set up in the district of Coochbehar immediately.
10. Regarding exchange of enclaves, Indian enclaves in Bangladesh and Bagladeshi enclaves in India be exchanged without further delay.
11. In respect of pre and post independent history of North Bengal a 'WHITE PAPER' regarding economic status, culture, population and ethnical identity of the original people of North Bengal be published immediately.

Appendix D

Memorandum submitted to the Prime Minister of India by Nikhil Kumar Ray, President of Kamtapur People's Party on 28.09.2005.

From

NIKHIL KUMAR RAY

President

Kamatapur People's Party

To

The Hon'ble Prime Minister

Govt. of India

New Delhi -= 110001

In Ref: Letter, Dated 28-09-2005

For New Kamatapur State

And for Recognition of Kamatapur language

Under VIII Schedule of the Constitution of India

MEMORANDUM

Sir,

Under the reasonable necessity and obligation, I compel to draw your sincere attention to the fact that the long standing demand for New Kamatapur State comprising of 6 District of North Bengal is insistent and compelling.

It is compelling because-

1. It is a demand that first initiated by Uttar Khanda Dal (UKD) in 1969 i.e. 39 years ago for emancipating the kamatees people from the tentacles of Bengal Tyrannism. For which one Gagen Roy, Jagadish Roy and many others sacrifice their life for the cause of separate state.
2. Kamatapur peoples party renewed the Andolan in the name of Kamatapuri Andolan in 1996. Again in 1999, thousands of people were arrested, raided, totured, jailed and hundreds of people were sacrifice their life for their cause of –
   - **(a)** New Kamatapur State
   - **(b)** Recognition of Kamatapur language, political, economical and cultural development of all the jatis and janajatis of the area concerned.
3. The colonial type exploitation, oppression and negligence should be stopped in North Bengal.
4. Massive influx of foreign Nationals should be indentified and evicted to stop the tensions born out of the struggles for mere survival and again to stop cross border terrorism, black marketing, dacoity, smuggling etc.
5. To stop rudimentary agriculture, massive poverty, endemic employment and to establish industry, agro-industry, agricultural-irrigation projects etc.
6. To stop cultural exploitation and to provide Kamatapuri Language and Kamatapuri cultural of their own.

7. To stop natural resource exploitation i.e. forest products, agricultural products, minerals, etc. in North Bengal.
8. To stop illegal and criminal activities and to maintain law and order situation, a separate state is compelling.
9. To fulfill urges and aspirations of Kamatees people for better identity in concerned area.
10. It is historically proper, geographically desirable, economically essential, constitutionally correct and legally justified. In conclusion it is your only judicious state-craft that can fulfill the urges and aspirations of the people of North Bengal carving out a New Kamatapur State comprising of Six districts of North Bengal namely Cooch Behar, Jalpaiguri, Darjeeling, Uttar Dinajpur, Dakshin Dinajpur and Malda under the article 3 of the constitution of India.

If the process of making separate state would not be allowed to start sharply, we have no other alternative than to lunch democratic movement to get justice and redress.

Thanking you in anticipation of your favourable action ____

Enclose:

(i) A Xerox copy of memorandum to the Prime Minister of India. Dated 28.09.2005

(ii) A Xerox copy of memorandum to the Minister of Home Affairs. Dated 28.9.2005

(iii) A Xerox copy of Mass deputation to the D. M. Dated 25.04.2005

(iv) A Xerox copy of memorandum to the Director General & Inspector General of Police, West Bengal, Dated: 27.06.2005

(v) A Xerox copy of memorandum to the Hon'ble Prime Minister, Govt. of India, Date: 06.01.1999

I Remain,

Yours faithfully

Nikhil Kumar Ray

President

Kamatapur People's Party

Appendix E

THE GREATER COOCH BEHAR PEOPLE'S ASSOCIATION

Central Committee

H.O.CHAKCHAKA, COOCH BEHAR

President :Nirmal Roy *General Secretary: Namita Barman*

Ref No.GCPA/ 0793/2016 *Date. 14/04/2016*

To

ShriRajnath Singh
The Hon'ble Home Minister
Govt. of India
New Delhi-110001

Sub :Regarding formation of Greater Cooch Behar State

Respected Sir,

On behalf of the Greater Cooch Behar Peoples' Association, we wish to draw your kind attention to our Prayer No.GCPA/460/2015 dated 11/12/2015 during our successfull meeting with your good self at your residence and subsequent issue of Govt. Press Release on the same date giving firm commitments to fulfill our demands. We enclose copies of the same for your ready reference, please.

2. It has been more than a month, we have not received any communication from the Govt. of India on the urgent and important issue of formation of separate Cooch Behar State within the framework of Indian Constitution or bring under the Union (Union Territory) by forming a high power expert committee. The people of erstwhile Greater Cooch Behar State are becoming impatient for the delay in fulfilling our justified demands. Assurances given late ShriSardarVallabhBhai Patel, then Home Minister during the merger in 1949, to protect the interests of our people and give socio-economic, cultural, linguistic and most importantly the democratic rights in real sense are still awaited to be fulfilled. In the meanwhile, sufferings of people of Cooch Behar are increasing day by day.

3. We, also submit our another important demand that as per the Merger Agreement and an assurance given by late ShriVapalPangunniMenon, then Adviser to the Govt. of India, Ministry of States, New Delhi on behalf of Union Govt. and Lt. Col. His Highness Maharaja Jagaddipandra Narayan BhupBahadur, then Maharaja of Cooch Behar State saying that "The Government will endeavour to associate the name of 'Narayan" with the Cooch Behar State Forces (which was famous as NarayaniSena) even after their absorption in the Indian Army". Therefore, you are requested to take the initiative to raise a 'Narayani' Regiment for the people of Cooch Behar as an infantry regiment in the Indian Army.

4. As per para (8) of V.P. Menon's D.O. No. F.15(19)-P49 dated the 30th August, 1949we also Submit our another important demand for Coronation Maharaja Sri SriAnanta Roy as President of DebutterTrust as per the Merger Agreement and assurance given by V.P. Menon, then adviser to the Govt. of India, Ministry of States Saying that "the management of the temples and Debutter Properties in the state may be entrusted to a Trust which Shall Consist of your Highness as President, 3 nominees of your Highness and 2 nominees of Govt. This Trust will be in charge of all temples in the State and will also administer the properties of the temples both inside and outside the State. In the event of the abolition of the zamindaris which are Debutter property Govt. will ensure that the Trust has adequate resources to fill its object."

Cont Page 2

//2//

5. Finally we also want to have the allotment theLand of Chakchaka ground from your good self for Construction of Rajbanshi Community hall. In every year birth day celebration of Vir Surya ViswaMahavirChila Roy, Madancumdav worship, Dashara etc. are celebrated in this field.

The Statue of Vir Surya ViswaMahavirChila Roy, a Cultural Stage have already been founded in the field of Chakchaka. The temple of Shiv Chandi is also in the field.

So we also request you to install the Statue of Vir Surya ViswaMahaVirChila Roy in the Parliament Complex.

Sir, we, therefore, request your good self to consider our justified demands as mentioned above and as mentioned in the prayer submitted by us to you on 11/12/2015 have already been recorded in your office.

With regards

Yours faithfully
NirmalRoy
President
The Greater Cooch Behar
People's Association
H.O. Chakchaka,Cooch Behar

Appendix F

THE GREATER COOCH BEHAR PEOPLE'S ASSOCIATION

Central Committee

H.O. CHAKCHAKA, COOCH BEHAR

President : Nirmal Roy *General Secretary: Namita Barman*

Ref No. GCPA/ 462/2016 *Date. 18/01/2016*

To

Shri Rajnath Singh
The Hon'ble Home Minister
Govt. of India
New Delhi-110001

Sub : Regarding formation of Greater Cooch Behar State

Respected Sir,

On behalf of the Greater Cooch Behar Peoples' Association, we wish to draw your kind attention to our Prayer No.GCPA/460/2015 dated 11/12/2015 during our successfull meeting with your good self at your residence and subsequent issue of Govt. Press Release on the same date giving firm commitments to fulfill our demands. We enclose copies of the same for your ready reference, please.

2. It has been more than a month, we have not received any communication from the Govt. of India on the urgent and important issue of formation of separate Cooch Behar State within the framework of Indian Constitution or bring under the Union (Union Territory) by forming a high power expert committee. The people of erstwhile Greater Cooch Behar State are becoming impatient for the delay in fulfilling our justified demands. Assurances given late Shri Sardar Vallabh Bhai Patel, then Home Minister during the merger in 1949, to protect the interests of our people and give socio-economic, cultural, linguistic and most importantly the democratic rights in real sense are still awaited to be fulfilled. In the meanwhile, sufferings of people of Cooch Behar are increasing day by day.

3. We, also submit our another important demand that as per the Merger Agreement and an assurance given by late Shri Vapal Pangunni Menon, then Adviser to the Govt. of India, Ministry of States, New Delhi on behalf of Union Govt. and Lt. Col. His Highness Maharaja Jagaddipendra Narayan Bhup Bahadur, then Maharaja of Cooch Behar State saying that "The Government will endeavour to associate the name of 'Narayan" with the Cooch Behar State Forces (which was famous as Narayani Sena) even after their absorption in the Indian Army". Therefore, you are requested to take the initiative to raise a 'Narayani' Regiment for the people of Cooch Behar as an infantry regiment in the Indian Army.

Sir, we, therefore, request your good self to consider our justified demands as mentioned above and as mentioned in the prayer submitted by us to you on 11/12/2015 without further delay.

With regards

Yours faithfully

Nirmal Roy
President
The Greater Cooch Behar
People's Association
H.O. Chakchaka,Cooch Behar

Copy for information to S.S. Ahluwalia, Member of Parliamnt from Darjeeling

Enclosures:

1. Copy of Prayer No.GCPA/460/2015 dated 11/12/2015
2. Copy of Govt. of India Press Release dated 11/12/2015

Appendix G

THE GREATER COOCH BEHAR PEOPLE'S ASSOCIATION

H.O. COOCH BEHAR

President : *Nirmal Roy*　　Central Committee　　Secretary : *Namita Barman*

Ref. No. G.C.P.A. (03)-09　　Date 24/03/09

From :
Kumari Namita Barman
General Secretary
The General Cooch Behar People's Association
Head Office : Cooch Behar.

To
Smt. Pratibha Devi Singh Patil
Her Excellency President of India,
Rastrapati Bhawan,
New Delhi - 110004

To
Dr. Monmohan Singh
The Prime Minister,
Govt. of India,
South Block,
New Delhi - 110001

To
The Home Minister,
Govt. of India,
New Delhi - 110011.

Subject :

A) Kind request to stop the Parliamentery election Processing of India / Over The Greater Cooch Behar Princely state as a 'C' camp state in the Indian Constitution adopted on 26th November, 1949.

B) To send the invitation letter on behalf of Govt. of India for the Representative nominated by the People of The Greater Cooch Behar State for the Indian Parliamentery administrative set-up.

C) To Provide with Suitable place for the qualified, responsible nominated representative from The Cooch Behar Princely State in the Indian Constituent Assembly unanimously
adopted on 26th November, 1949.

D) To execute the Indian Constitutional Processing with permission for the structure of care-taker Ministry by The Greater Cooch Behar People's Association in The Greater Cooch Behar 'C' camp state.

Respected Madam / Sir,

We, on behalf of The Greater Cooch Behar People's Association as well as the Ethnic and Bonafied people of The Greater Cooch Behar State have the honour to inform you through our modest request that India became free on 15th August in 1947 through the non-violent movement led by Mahatma Gandhi by dint of the Indian Independence Act came to effect on 18th July, 1947 pased from the British Parliament dividing India into two dominions by the name of India and Pakistan. Pakistan was subsequently geographically divided into two parts by the name of East Pakistan (Bangladesh) and West Pakistan (Pakistan) In between of these two parts India stands. In the same way India was also geographi cally parted into two parts by the name of East India and West India. In bewteen of these two parts of India Cooch Behar had an own existance as a separate independent country, ruled by His Highness Maharaja. The British Govt. tactfully occupied some areas from Maharaja of the then Cooch Behar in from 1773 to 1902 A.D. through various agreements. Those occupied areas were handed over to His Highness on 18th July, 1947 by vertue of {(7/1) b} Act of Indian Independence ending the Agreement.

Pandit Jawharlal Nehru, Prime Minister and Sarder Ballav Bhai Patel, Home Minister of the then India had negotiated with the Maharaja Sri Sri Jagaddipendra Narayan Bhup Bahadur of the princely state of Cooch Behar regarding the subject of Merger and in exchange of both their opinion the erstwhile Cooch Behar State was merged with India and the Maharaja, Sri Sri Jagaddipendra Narayan Bhup Bahadur has handed over the land of Cooch Behar to us at the time of Cooch Behar Merger maintaining our tradditional common peace and harmony upohlding the honour of The Cooch Behar Princely State as we have liability and responsibility which had been bestowed to us by birth.

The agreement was signed by V.P. Menon, the

Governor General of India and the Maharaja Sri Sri Jagaddipendra Narayan Bhup Bahadur. We readily accepted the agreement with pride and gladness. As per as the Merger V.I. Nanjappa the chief commissioner of India handed over the administration taking from the Maharaja of Cooch Behar princely state to the Govt. of India on 12th Sept, 1949. The Govt. of India peacefully took over the charge with liability and responsibility securing the stock of finance along with all sorts of asset of The Cooch Behar State. Accordingly The Cooch Behar was recognised as a 'C' category state of India as per as the Indian constitution adopted on 26th November 1949 and was placed in the 1st schedule of the Indian constitution. On 1st January 1950 the erstwhile Cooch Behar Princely state was marged with West Bengal by dint of the British India Provincial Autonomous Act. 1935. Subsequently two representatives from The Cooch Behar State were nominated by the then Governor for the legislative assembly of West Bengal. The two representativs were (i) Satish Chandra Roy Singh Sarkar (ii) Umesh Chandra Mondal.

In 1956 the 'C' category states in the list of 1st Schedule of the Indian Constitution was ommitted throught the seventh amendment. It was from then the people of The Greater Cooch Behar State were treated badly by the rulers in power / with the reparcable/ confusional activities of the Indian constitution. Today we are really distressed and painfully wounded by the ruthlessness and diplomacy of Politics. Losing mental, Physical, financial, social, religious, geographical balance along with our common good will and harmony, we are in great danger. Assimilating with the newly set-up India framed, by Mahatma Gandhi we are at the extreme point of our social as well as our national existance.

Today we are in great poverty and searching for food, shelter including every thing necessary for our existance leaving The Cooch Behar State, our mother land we are bound to lead our lives under the foot of human civilisation in different parts of India. We are living in such a way as if we have no self-prestige and honour which was bestowed to us by birth. We had been living by birth in the land of The Cooch Behar which was separate independent country and belong to the Rajbanshi Community of The Cooch Behar Kingdom. We do not know the constitutional deplomatic political set-up of the then newly framed India. We have been compelled to lead our livelihood which is about to be destroyed from the real existance of the then princely state of Cooch Behar. We have been merged with the Indian Territory on 28th August, 1949 to live happily and peacefully altogether sharing the happiness and sorrow to each other as human race of the country.

History says we are the sons ofthis land and since the birth of human race and civilisation we had been living in this land. Our administratie system is based on monarchysm. We are (state of King) innocent of the system of democratic set-up of India, we became able to realise the rules and regulation processing of the Indian democratic civilisation through the matter in details as follows.

It is quoted in the Indian constitution that one seat was decided comprising the population of10 lakh to form the constituent assembly. Each province and each Indian state or group of states were alloted the total number of seats proportional to their respective populations roughly in the ratio of on eto a million. As a result, the provinces were to elect 292 members while the Indian states were alloted a minimum of 93 seats.

It is remarkable that after consulting the procedure of nomination from the autonomous territory nominated person is sent to form the constituent aasembly. But at that time there was no provision for representation from the erst while Cooch Behar State. On 29th August 1947 a drafting committee under the chairmanship of Dr. B.R. Ambedkar was appointed in the form of draft constitution of India on the 29th November 1949 on which date the constitution received signature of the president of the Assembly and was declared passed. The erst while Cooch Behar state was enlisted as a 'C' category state in the first schedule of the Indian Constitution unanimously. On 1st January, 1950 without taking consent of the people of the Cooch Behar 'C' Camp state the Governor-General of India merged the Cooch Behar 'C' Camp state with West Bengal which is recognised as a 'A' category state in the 1st Schedule of the Indian Constitution by dint of the British-India Act 1935.

In 1956 through the seventh amendent of the Indian Constitution 'C' category states of the 1st Schedule were omitted. But the question is, including The Greater Cooch Behar State in the 'C' Category of the

1st Schedule, the same state (Cooch Behar State) was merged by the Governor with West Bengal with the help of British India provincial assimilation Act. 1935. If the Governor-General can assimilate The Cooch Behar 'C' Caterogy state with the 'A' Category state name ly West Bengal by dint of 1935 British India Act, what was the use of Cooch Behar marger-agreement with India on 28th August, 1949? The erst while Cooch Beharstate was enlisted as a 'C' Category state in the 1st Schedule of the Indian Constitution adopted on 26th November, 1949. In 1956 through the seventh amendment by the Indian parliament the 'C' Category states in the first schedule were subsequently omitted. Has the Governor General any such authentic power to change and amend the Indian constitution?

If he had no such authentic power in the constitution, on what ground did he include the 'C' category Cooch Behar state in the 'A' category state of West Bengal? If the Governor has any kind of authentic power to change any part of the Indian Constitution, what was the use of constitutional amendement by the members of the parliament to omit the 'C' Category states in 1956?

If the Governor had no such authentic power to omit the 'C' Category state in the Indian Constitution by way of 1935 Act. Since 26th November, 1949 upto 1956 our Greater Cooch Behar State would have been existed / established as a 'C' Category state as per as the Indian Constitution.

Despite of Being as a 'C' Category State in the Indian state how and why the administration of West

Bengal which is still now recognised as a 'A' category state is running over The Greater Cooch Behar State? If the erst while Cooch Behar state would have been merged with West Bengal, how and why the two candidates from The Cooch Behar Princely State were nominated by the Governor of West Bengal for the Legislative Assembly of the State (West Bengal) in 1950?

In case of 'A' category state of West Bengal there was no consitutional authentic power to send nominated representatives to the legislative assembly.

The Indian constitution has given the autonomous territorial state to nominate representative from the state as it thinks fit.

Hence we think, since the merger-agreement between The Cooch Behar State and India our erst while Cooch Behar State is out side the Indian Constitution.

Federation and authonomy

While under all the previous Government of India acts, the Government of India was unitary, the Act of 1935 [prescribed a federation, taking the provinces and Indian states as units. But it was optional for the Indian states to join the federation and since the Rulers of the Indian States never gave their consent, the federation envisaged by the Act of 1935 never came into being.

Place of Indian states in the
federal schemes proposed by
the Government of India Act. 1935

It is needless to elaborate the details of the plan of

1935, for as has been stated earlier the accession of the Indian states to the proposed federation never came true, and this part of that Act was finally abandoned in 1939, when World War II broke out.

When Sir stafford cripps came to India with his plan, it was definitely unders tood that the plan proposed by him would be confined to setting the political destinies of British India and that the Indian states would be left free to retain their seperate status.

India and The Cooch Behar State are related to each other only for the Merger- Agreement between India and Cooch Behar.

The Indian constitution itself says if any province is merged with Indian territory the Indian constituent Assembly must be signed by te representative of that country.

If it is not done, The Indian constitution will be forcefully impossed upon the people of the country. As there was no nominated representative from The Cooch Behar state in the secular, democratic, federal constitutent Assembly of the Indian Constitution, we feel that the Indian constitution had been forcefully imposed upon the people of the Cooch Behar princely state.

There is no election processing in the monarchical system of The Cooch Behar State. The king of our Cooch Behar state form the ministerial assembly.

On 11th Sept, 1949 the Home Minister Sardar Ballav Bhai Patel on behalf of the Govt. of India promised the people of the Cooch Behar, "I hope therefore, that the people of Cooch Behar will work with sigle mindeness and devotion to duty as a united team for their own betterment and to achieve their due place in the political and administrative set-up of India." Inconnection with this promise two representatives from Cooch Behar were nominated by the Governor of then West Bengal and allowed to represent in the Legislative assembly in Kolkata. Does it mean that the legislative assembly of West Bengal administer all over India? Does the Legislative Assembly of West Bengal represent the parliamentary administrative system of India?

On 11th Sept. 1949 the Home Minister Sarder Ballab Bhai Patel on behalf of the Govt. of India has promised, the people of the Cooch Behar state will be allowed to achieve their place in political and administrative set-up of India.

As per as the promise made by the Govt.of India, in the event of Provision for the nominated representative from The Greater Cooch Behar state to be allowed in the administrative set-up of India, it will be legal as per as the constitution of The Cooch Behar as well as that of India.

We shall therefore send constitutionally responsible and qualified representatives nominated from The Greater Cooch Behar Princely State to the parliamentary administrative system of India in proper time through you after the forth-coming Loksabha election of India 2009 being over.

Madam / Sir, We on behalf of the people of The Greater Cooch Behar State through The Greater Cooch Behar People's Association therefore modestly inform you that the Loksabha Election for the constitutional parliament of India in North Bengal comprising Cooch Behar,

Jalpaiguri, Darjeeling, North & South Dinajpur districts of West Bengal is going to be held on 30th April 2009. The above quoted areas are the constitutional areas of the proposed Greater Cooch Behar State. You have already been informed earlier regarding this matter in our prayer in details to impliment the Merger Agreement.

You have been already informed through The Greater Cooch Behar People's Association regarding this matter in our prayer in defails requesting to implement the Merger Agreement made on 28th August 1949. The above quoted Cooch Behar state was recognised as a 'C' category state in the original constitution of India adopted on 26th November, 1949 and enlisted in the 1st Schedule of the Indian Constitution.

We have therefore decided not to participate in the constitutional parliamentary election system of India and send representatives from The Greater Cooch Behar State to the Parliamentary administrative system of India, Parliament Bhawan.

If the processing of democratic parliamentary Loksabha election of India over The Greater Cooch Behar State is held, it will be unconstitutional activities for the constitution of The Cooch Behar State as well as that of India.

Therefore you are modestly requested to stop the Indian constitutional Loksabha Election (2009) processing with in a very short time that will be unconstitutional for The Greater Cooch Behar Princely State and to exceute the Indian Constitutional processing with permission for the structure of caretaker Ministry by The

Greater Cooch Behar People's Association in The Greater Cooch Behar 'C' Camp state.

If the nominated representatives on behalf of the people of The Greater Cooch Behar Princely State achieve their place in the Indian constituent Assembly through the amendment of the Indian Constitution and the Indian constitution allows the people of The Greater Cooch Behar state to have their place through the representatives of The Greater Cooch Behar Princely State we shall have no any constitutional objection to accept the Indian constitution.

The Indian Constitution will be glorious and ideal for ever to the people of The Greater Cooch Behar Princely State.

We have fully belief in the ideal of Mahatma Gandhi, the father of nation of India and also in his ideal Indian Adninistrative system that the socio-economic development of the people of The Cooch Behar Princely State will be established through the implementation of The Cooch Behar Princely State will be established through the implementation of The Greater Cooch Behar Marger Agreement by the continuation of Dharna since 28th August 2006 at the historical Jantar-Manter in New Delhi.

With regards

Yours faithfully

Kumari Namita Barman
General Secretary
The Greater Cooch Behar People's Association

❖❖❖❖❖